ADULT EDUCATION IN THE PARISH

D1453904

ADULT EDUCATION IN THE PARISH

A PRACTICAL HANDBOOK

Kathy D. Rucker

St. Anthony Messenger Press

CINCINNATI, OHIO

Nihil Obstat: Rev. Hilarion Kistner, O.F.M.
Rev. Robert L. Hagedorn

Imprimi Potest: Rev. Jeremy Harrington, O.F.M.
Provincial

Imprimatur: +James H. Garland, V.G.
Archdiocese of Cincinnati
December 1, 1989

The *nihil obstat* and *imprimatur* are a declaration that a book is considered to be free from doctrinal or moral error. It is not implied that those who have granted the *nihil obstat* and *imprimatur* agree with the contents, opinions or statements expressed.

Cover and book design by Julie Lonneman

ISBN 0-86716-125-6

Preface

Even a small book cannot come into being without help from many people. I want to thank Monsignor Richard Allen, my former pastor, for his unshakable trust and vision in inviting me to lead his parish staff in the area of adult education. Sharing leadership with laity continues to challenge many clergy and I am grateful for the way Father Allen supported his parish adult education team—with wholehearted enthusiasm for our plans and a place in the parish budget for this important ministry to adults.

Team effort is essential to adult education. Because of this, I owe a large debt of gratitude to the many adults who served so generously on our team during the years I worked as adult education director. These people, by their tireless work and competency in educational ministry to adults, proved many times over how we are "church" for each other. Working with such dedicated volunteers was a rare and unforgettable privilege. Two team members, Dr. Tim Kute and Sister Jackie Staub, S.S.J., served for six years providing countless hours of direction and leadership.

Two other members of St. Leo's Adult Faith Development Team deserve special mention because of their roles as teachers. Both taught by their lives well lived more than by any single thing they said. Marge Tyndall brought dignity and gracious hospitality to the people who knew her. She worked to create this same spirit of welcome among those she met in church. Ken Brennan's good judgment and loyalty to his friends supported the parish team through many years of his leadership. Both savored lives of prayer and lived out faithfulness to the spirit of the gospel. Their devotion to family and friends and their courage in facing death make the lessons we learned from them especially memorable.

I want to thank those friends who encouraged me to put in book form some of the ideas we gained from ministry to adult learners. Father Ken Boyack, C.S.P., who directed such wonderful programs for adults while he served with the Paulist Fathers in North Carolina, made time to read this manuscript and offer constructive criticism. Dorothea Dlabal, Mary Jo McBride and Father Frank McNulty also offered their careful reading and helpful comments. Father Lou Bonacci, S.J., assisted with some final details and Edith Thomas provided friendship and important reminders of what we were all about. Thanks also to Dr. Fred Horton for encouraging me to write this book. The book's shortcomings are the author's and in no way reflect the judgment of these good people.

Most importantly, I want to thank my family for the sacrifices they made during my years of directing adult education work and writing this book. They ate at more church potluck suppers than I can count and offered hospitality to frequent out-of-town speakers who graced our own dinner table. I hope Tom, Jr., and Marion will remember the excitement their parents felt about the Church rather than the numerous late-night meetings during those busy years. My husband, Tom, supported every part of this effort with his love and uncomplaining generosity. I would wish the blessing of this kind of support for every lay minister.

Kathy D. Rucker
February 9, 1990

Contents

Introduction   1

CHAPTER ONE:
Gathering a Team   3

CHAPTER TWO:
Getting Ideas, Planning the Programs   13

CHAPTER THREE:
Publicity—Spreading the Good Word   23

CHAPTER FOUR:
Gaining Support   33

CHAPTER FIVE:
Hospitality—More Than Punch and Cookies   43

CHAPTER SIX:
The Care and Feeding of Speakers   51

CHAPTER SEVEN:
Using Films and Videotapes Effectively   57

CHAPTER EIGHT:
Choosing Criteria for Success   63

CHAPTER NINE:
Spirituality and the Adult Educator   71

Afterword   81

APPENDIX A:
Sample Evaluation Form   83

APPENDIX B:
Resource Guide   85

Dedication

To my parents, Dorothea and Luke Dlabal,
on their fiftieth wedding anniversary, October 18, 1989,
and to Tom, Tom, Jr., and Marion for their love

Introduction

The telephone rings insistently. When I pick up the receiver, a voice on the other end explains that a group of six people in her church is trying to form an adult education committee. The person admits half-reluctantly, half-proudly that she has been elected chairperson for the group. She wants to know if I have any suggestions for programs or for what they need to do. She has heard that I have headed the adult education efforts for my parish for several years. In short, could I help?

This book takes on the challenging question posed by my telephone caller. Each of us who has served in any way as a midwife for the emerging movement of adult education in the Church has plunged into a ministry for which few guidebooks exist. One reason for the dearth of books on parish-based adult education is that each parish operates within a unique set of resources, finances and circumstances. No general guides, therefore, could explain exactly how to make adult education flourish in a particular parish. Besides, parishioners would not want a program to be decided upon by someone who did not understand and value the particular gifts of their local church community—and rightly so.

As some of us, however, have faced the challenges of setting up committees, determining goals, publicizing our programs, struggling to motivate increasing numbers of adults and evaluating our experiences, we have accumulated some information which could help other groups facing similar work.

This book has evolved from our successes, our failures and a desire to share what can help those who are just beginning to develop parish programs for adults. I hope my writing will encourage you as you take up the joyful midwifery of bringing to life many varied and attractive opportunities for adults who want to grow in their faith.

Innumerable small tasks go into the building of an effective ministry in adult faith development. This book identifies many of those tasks. A checklist at the end of each chapter reviews main points and can serve as a short double-check on the work accomplished in local planning sessions. I also have added the names of some helpful books in which readers can find more detailed information. Many of these fine books treat certain topics in depth, and I am indebted to their authors for continuing to nourish my understanding.

Above all, I want the reader to understand that I intend for this book to serve as an *introductory* guide because, in a sense, all who work in this frontier territory of adult faith development are pioneers who are also shapers of the ministry.

Since Vatican II, the American Church has increasingly emphasized the Church as the *People of God*. This image is a dynamic one. It suggests people "on the move," interpreting their traditions and gospel for their own times. What nourishes and sustains us, the People of God, as we wander through the deserts of our life experiences and climb to the peaks of new human awareness? Can the Church with all its wonderful resources be there for adults moving from one passage to another? Can we identify the needs of the Church of the future and prepare ourselves to live and celebrate within that community?

Adult educators live and work with these exciting questions. My prayer is that through our work in adult faith development and education we continue to feed the human spirit that hungers for the truth which brings us closer to the Source of all truth.

CHAPTER ONE

Gathering a Team

*It was said about an old man that he endured seventy weeks of
fasting, eating only once a week. He asked God about certain words
in the Holy Scripture, but God did not answer him. Then he said to
himself: Look, I have put in this much effort, but I haven't made any
progress. So now I will go to see my brother, and ask him. And
when he had gone out, closed the door and started off, an angel of
the Lord was sent to him, and said: Seventy weeks of fasting have
not brought you near to God. But now that you are humbled
enough to go to your brother, I have been sent to you to reveal the
meaning of the words. Then the angel explained the meaning which
the old man was seeking, and went away.*
                                    —*Yushi Nomura*, Desert Wisdom

W hy do so many educators recommend creating a team
for adult faith development? That is a key question
and a good place to begin.

In the Bible, we do not have to look far for examples of
a team approach. Jesus constantly worked with groups. His
apostles and disciples participated in his ministry. Forming
a group was also the first thing the disciples did after his
death. Although the followers of Jesus didn't have a mission
statement or even a set of goals for the coming year,
instinctively they "grouped" in the Upper Room. Perhaps,
too, the frequent gatherings reported in Acts stem from a
sense that no one person had all of the faith; no one person,
not even Mary, had all of the vision or grace for the whole
emerging Church. Together, however, the disciples could
support one another's flagging faith. They could remind one
another of the stories of Jesus and help to develop life in the

new communities. They learned that they could pool their talents: The preachers could preach, the planners could plan and the deacons could oversee the distribution of alms.

Working as a team can be an expression of faith and a witness to it. When people gather together in the name of the Lord to reflect on the needs of their community, they count on the promise of protection and guidance from the Holy Spirit and they carry the memory of a longstanding tradition of faith development.

The team approach to adult education can be enormously beneficial to a pastor. Incredible demands are placed on most pastors' schedules. Often his life is filled with liturgical duties and a blur of meetings and private conferences. An adult education team can multiply the effectiveness of his ministry by seeking his input for program ideas and evaluation and then doing the detailed planning. The pastor's openness to sharing responsibility with his parishioners in this work can unlock the door to wonderful ways his ministry can be extended beyond the limits of his own 24-hour day.

An obvious benefit of collaboration is the possibility of drawing on a whole gamut of talents in planning and executing programs. Our team managed to recruit a photographer who had limited time but a real desire to help. When we planned our brochures, his expertise in layout and his eye for design proved invaluable. When we needed to boost our public relations effort and tell the story of what the RCIA (Rite of Christian Initiation of Adults) group, for example, had experienced, what better way to do it than with photographs showing the various rites, celebrations and impromptu get-togethers?

Another team member, a psychiatrist, was skilled in leading groups in stress management, positive visualization and meditation exercises. While others developed the curriculum or designed tools for evaluation of programs, he was able to plan and teach several popular courses in psychospiritual growth and serve as a local resource person for follow-up.

When a new budget item comes up for discussion by

parish finance officers, a committee member skilled in financial matters can help explain how well-developed adult education programs are both affordable and necessary. Our parish team benefited on numerous occasions from the expertise of a certified public accountant who assisted with budget preparation. He also regularly helped clarify our budget requests to the finance committee.

"What gift does this person bring to our group?" A wise team keeps looking for people who can bring unusual talents to help plan and build good programs. Team members need to stay open to all kinds of creative possibilities for using people's talents and skills. Many parishioners are eager to help out, but they have not heard anyone in ministry affirm that they have something special to give. Identifying and inviting gifted people is especially important.

Building Respect, Care and Concern

When a group rather than an individual takes charge of planning, executing and evaluating faith development programs, there is no room for superstars. A team is a community which both suffers the setbacks and owns the victories. In a group of this sort, people graciously give their service whether it be heading a fund drive or baking cookies for a reception. A payoff in all of this is the friendships that build.

Care and concern for one another grow within the team. A bond of friendship encourages members to babysit for each other's children, enjoy a night out together, celebrate birthdays together, visit each other when sick and take meals to the family of a hospitalized team member. I view this as both a natural and healthy outgrowth of team ministry and a microcosm of Church.

Loving care is surely a sign that God's Spirit has taken root in the community and this Spirit enlivens people to act in creative ways. Such care is no small accident of parish ministry; rather, it is central to the purpose of adult faith development: to assist people to understand and live their

5

faith commitments. If we want to enable people to live more completely the caring values that Jesus tried to teach, we must first recognize our need to live out that message ourselves. The team must model the behavior or goal which it seeks to bring about.

The concept of team invites us to move away from programs which are dominated by one leader who develops classes for the good of others who need to be changed in some way. Dialogue among the people for whom the ministry is designed is mandatory in adult faith development. We need to avoid the kind of adult education classes which are run by someone who hopes to indoctrinate those who have not had the advantage of a seminary, college or ministry education background.

Some contemporary movements in parish life and renewal, namely the RCIA and the RENEW program, center intrinsically on group experience. They are processes rather than programs. For their success they need to draw on the talents of the entire community. Both the RCIA and RENEW call for a well-established team ministry on which further community can be built.

At one point our parish wanted to link the adult education programs with other existing parish activities and groups. As a result we adopted a policy of co-sponsoring at least two offerings each year with other parish organizations. This allowed us to gain new friends with other kinds of loyalties to the parish and to expand our offerings as we were joined by other chairpersons and assistants.

Admittedly, this method often means some compromise in controlling exactly how the educational event unfolds, but it also broadens our understanding of the commitment of other parishioners and of how much their goals parallel ours. It also states again that we have no room for superstars in the guise of an individual or a group.

Finding Balances

The ideal size of a team for adult education depends on circumstances. The size of ours has fluctuated over the years. Our largest board included 15 people. At that time we were trying an organizational plan whereby each team member would be responsible for working on two programs or projects during the calendar year; hence the need for a larger board to fill the organizational substructure of the committee. We realized, however, that 15 was too large for good communication. After paring the team to eight, we found we had a comfortable working group which could draw easily on the knowledge and contributions of each member.

We also found it helpful to get representation from all segments of the parish. For instance, if the average age of your group tends to be 40-ish, be sure to recruit representation from both the young and the elderly. Include both the married and the single. It is important to consider all groups, especially if a parish is large and dominated by many families with school-age children. Some of the most enthusiastic support for our programs has come from the young singles and from the senior citizens. Older parish members have more leisure—sometimes for the first time in their lives—to pursue some growth issues and theological study they have always wanted to do. They also bring knowledge and experience to a team.

Some degree of religious homogeneity is also desirable. That is not to say people with differing devotional lives or theological ideas cannot be effective team members. Yet, if the discrepancies are too great, the team can get so wound up in internal struggles over these differences that the goal of ministering to a larger group within the parish can be lost.

Nurturing Team Members

All people need ongoing care and nurturing. Adult education team members are no exception. A wise director will plan enrichment events especially for the team. A universally accepted management axiom is "people pursue personal payoffs." Even though the "duty ethic" might have once motivated parishioners to *sacrifice* their time in parish service, people today are legitimately expecting to get something out of such service. Team enrichment should involve some days away annually, if possible, not only for goal setting and discussion of the team's mission but simply for the ongoing nurture of the team itself. Most volunteers who lead busy lives managing families and work responsibilities, as well as church commitments, appreciate time for reflection during a day away or an annual retreat weekend.

Another important means of nurturing team members is giving them printed resources. A subscription to *Catholic Update* (published by St. Anthony Messenger Press), for instance, for each person is not a costly item, and it provides ongoing stimuli each month on a topic of contemporary interest. In addition, if the parish has budgeted money for library materials, the director can make these available to the team first, as a kind of bonus for their service. Team members are often hungry for ongoing spiritual reading.

Special occasions provide opportunities for the team to celebrate together. A milestone birthday, someone's promotion, or the ending of another good year in adult education work can be a cause for a treat or a meal together. In this kind of sharing, we keep company with Jesus who ate, drank and celebrated with his disciples and the people he loved. Surely the relaxing times Jesus shared with his disciples contributed to the bond which eventually formed that first committed, although hesitant, Church.

Spending time in festivity and celebration cannot be emphasized enough. Our space-age technology creates a vacuum in personal encounter. In our high-tech society computers, instead of telephone operators, give directions, numbers, information and a "listening ear." In addition the rugged individualism that has so characterized us as Americans also contributes to a sense of isolation. We often pride ourselves on having earned the amount of privacy, independence and financial security that allows us to decide whether or not to commit ourselves to anything. We can easily isolate ourselves and eventually experience a loneliness which we feel even within our Church.

Since Church offers community, a sense of belonging, the ministry team must model community and show its care and concern for its own members as well as for the people it serves. The payoff is that team members know that they can depend on other friends in the Christian community, these eight or 10 people who call themselves the adult faith development team. Team members usually feel a sense of belonging to Church as they facilitate community for others.

People on the team also need to know that when their interest wanes or the circumstances of their lives change, they are free to leave the team gracefully. Many who have been volunteers in the Church for a while consciously shy away from saying "yes" to any involvement that looks as if it will demand time right up to the moment of their last breath. Directors and team members need to maintain the kind of hospitable attitude that allows people to come and go freely. Team and other volunteers need to know that whatever time they can give will be gratefully received. We have had many team members come and go and all of them contributed something unique while they were with us. One member served with us only four months, but in that time she developed a task plan form that we continue to use when we plan a new series or program.

The other side of that openness to a person's leaving the ministry is, of course, a watchful eye for new people to be invited aboard. In a large parish where many members seldom know the people who sit next to them at Mass, identifying potential team members can be a challenge. That is why collaboration with groups such as a newcomers' welcoming committee and a family life commission is crucially important. Ideally team members should be at the newcomers' coffees and potluck suppers to help welcome people; they should also ask for some time on the agenda during the CCD or parish council meetings to make their ministry known to people in each of those groups. One of our best team members came forward to offer his services after hearing a brief talk at the initial CCD gathering in the fall. He was a classics professor at the local university, and his knowledge of classical and *koine'* Greek enormously enriched our Sunday morning Bible study while he was with us. Most of the time, however, we need to invite people to participate in the planning team's activities.

I have found that having lunch or coffee with prospective members works better as orientation than sending an information sheet. New team members will certainly need copies of reports and previous brochures, but most people join the team partly for their own social needs and partly to give of their time to the Church. I think we must respect this worthwhile mixture of motives and realize that the gift of personal presence in orientation and recruitment of the team is essential.

Sharing Wealth

Jesus has told us to share what we have with our sisters and brothers who have less. Unfortunately we can easily stereotype the poor as those people who frequent the soup kitchen or need help from a crisis control ministry. Or we may inventory our own wealth only in terms of how much we can offer others financially. We can overlook the richness of living in a parish that is blessed with personnel and media resources to conduct special programs. The Gospel calls us to share this kind of wealth with other parishes who may not be as fortunate. I would even go so far as to say that we have an obligation to dialogue with members of other parishes on how we can cooperatively serve their needs, and ours, too. When we collaborate with other parishes it is important to recognize that this doesn't mean that a parish rich in resources helps those poor people across town. Rather, members of both parishes meet in a spirit of openness. Both groups ask what they have to bring to a collaborative effort and what they stand to receive from the same effort. Neither patronizing attitudes nor pretentiousness has a place in the important work of adult faith development.

Checklist

Does your team represent the various ages and lifestyles of your parishioners?

In what ways does your team function as a model of Church?

What does your team do for renewal and enrichment?

How do you celebrate together and build rapport?

How do you welcome new members?

What happens when a member leaves the team?

Author's Annotated Bibliography

Coughlin, Kevin. *Motivating Adults for Religious Education*. Washington, D.C.: National Conference of Diocesan Directors of Religious Education—CCD, 1976. A valuable research paper which treats the causes and offers some remedies for motivational problems in adult growth opportunities. Realistic approach.

DeBoy, James J. *Getting Started in Adult Religious Education*. New York: Paulist Press, 1979. An excellent guide to the concept of adults managing their own planning for adult religious education. It offers a step-by-step guide to setting up a parish team and for designing goals and objectives.

Downs, Thomas. *The Parish as Learning Community*. New York: Paulist Press, 1979. This book discusses in depth the concept of a team model for the church and its importance for adult learning. A valuable resource.

Girziatis, Loretta. *The Church as Reflecting Community.* Mystic, Conn.: Twenty-Third Publications, 1977. Chapters Three and Four deal with recruiting and training a planning team.

CHAPTER TWO

Getting Ideas, Planning the Programs

In this world no one rules by mere love; if you are but amiable, you are no hero; to be powerful, you must be strong, and to have dominion you must have a genius for organizing.

—John Henry Newman

Many writers on adult education suggest that the best way to start a parish-based program is to take an extensive survey of parishioners' needs for spiritual and educational growth. A number of parishes and dioceses have developed inventories to accomplish this. I must say, right up front, that I do not usually work from a questionnaire. Why not? Don't I believe that such a parish survey could provide some valuable data? Yes, I do. Parish surveys give the person in the pew a chance to be heard and an opportunity to have a stake in the planning process.

Extensive surveys, however, hold inherent dangers. If the parish is large, the team will glean far more ideas for programs than it can begin to implement. Of course, the team can only respond to suggestions within limited resources: the budget, time for programs, team members' time and available speakers, facilitators and media resources. If most of the ideas cannot be used in the near future, many parishioners will feel frustrated. Some will complain that their responses weren't considered important. ("Wasn't my idea good enough?" "They are just interested in their own agenda anyway.")

Launching a major survey in a large parish requires

much time and energy. Although the team may gather tons of data, it will be able to use only a fraction of it effectively. Members may invest significant blocks of time in gathering an insignificant amount of useful information.

Suggestions for prophetic new directions for adult education sometimes do come from surveys. They cannot all be followed, however, because Church documents call for certain major adult education undertakings which compete for the parish resources. The RCIA is one example. The team must consider the Church directives first while prioritizing. Again, what the team chooses may be different from the most popular or creative suggestions on the survey.

Sources of Ideas for Planning

In our first years of ministry, our team voted down a total parish survey in favor of simpler methods of choosing what to sponsor. We start with an honest appraisal of our own desires for enrichment opportunities. If some team members are eager for a given process or topic, if a climate of honest sharing has been established and if the team has a broad representation of age and experience, chances are that the issues which come from the team itself will provide timely and valuable suggestions on what to offer. "What is my biggest challenge in trying to live out the Gospel?" usually elicits a wealth of potential topics from the team.

If you have a parish library, or even a small bookshelf of printed materials and tapes, the checkout cards will provide information about who is interested in what. Records from the parish book rack will reveal which titles intrigue people enough to buy or borrow them. Three popular titles in our church library are Marjorie Holmes' *I've Got to Talk to Somebody, God*, Leo Buscaglia's *Love* and Richard McBrien's *Catholicism*. If, knowing this, we focus our offerings on an exegesis of the Epistle to the Hebrews, we will not be swimming in the mainstream of people's interest.

Polling parish committees also can provide fruitful insights on some of the most pressing pastoral needs.

Important feedback can come from a simple conversation with committee heads or from attending a brief portion of a scheduled meeting to ask for some specific information or opinions. In these situations asking several specific questions will yield better results than holding a vague open-it-up-to-the-floor discussion.

If you ask opinions at a meeting, you also may have a chance to advertise your other programs. You may want to take a tip from marketers and employ the "focus group" technique. Ask your listeners how specific programs in the past met their needs. Even if a reaction to a program is indifferent or hostile, you are giving people a chance to vent their feelings so they can begin to hear again the message for future offerings.

If you are serious about getting people's honest reactions, you will win support. Most people light up when they realize that their personal views will be taken seriously. We discovered how true this is while we were planning a parish retreat. We needed to give our retreat director a list of issues that people identify as central to their spiritual lives. At the parish council and education commission meetings, we asked each member to reflect on the biggest challenge each found in leading a Christian life. They wrote down their ideas with or without identifying themselves and passed them in. We noticed later that an unusually large number of people from both groups participated in the retreat. People do like to be asked for their opinions.

Do consider carefully any feedback you receive from those who fill in evaluation sheets at the end of a program or series. These comments are especially valuable because they come from people who take time to participate. These people are serious about growing in their faith. We have found that these evaluation sheets *could* provide enough suggestions for all of our future programs.

The parish priests can also provide valuable observations and information. Their leadership position gives them a unique perspective on people's personal growth issues. And sometimes pressing concerns come to their attention in counseling sessions. When soliciting information from the priests, however, it should be clear that the team is gathering data for planning, not asking them to decide what the team should sponsor. The role of the adult faith development team as the leaders in planning and implementing activities must be preserved. Be sure, however, to follow up your meeting by keeping the pastor and parish staff informed at each stage of the planning process. A pastor, especially, generally likes to know what is happening even though he cannot attend every meeting. A wise team keeps all channels of communication open.

Watching Current Trends

Stay abreast of current trends in television, film and the popular press. In *The Religious Education of Adults*, Leon McKenzie warns, "Educational programs for adults that are 'churchy,' developed by educators who are possessed of a thoroughly 'churchy' consciousness, will appeal mainly to adults who are inclined to be 'churchy' in their outlook. If religious educators wish to broaden the appeal of their programs, they must come to terms with the values and orientations of those adults I categorize as contemporary."

The religious educator who does not follow this advice can find himself or herself in a safe bubble of church talk insulated from the daily life most parishioners experience. Avoid this security at all costs. It will be lethal to the adult program. Staying abreast of the news and the arts can help offset the temptation to encourage "churchaholism" in the team or parishioners.

Although your program will take place in church, the topic need not be the history of the Church or the lives of the saints. People appreciate programs which will help them to meet needs and solve problems. One problem that surfaced among team members was that of time pressures robbing them of a sense of the joy of living. Time for prayer, or just time to relax with the family, too often seemed to evaporate in the press of other obligations. So we asked a professional from a local university's business school to give a time-management workshop. Although participation was good, some parishioners questioned the value of including such a secular-sounding topic in our fall series. After the team read the feedback sheets and evaluated the event, however, they decided that this program was right on the money in ministering to people's real needs.

Obviously effective planning depends on the team's sensitivity to its potential learners. When you have collected enough data—through evaluation, formal questionnaires or informal polls—you are ready for the next phase of the process. The planning team can now meet and begin to shape the programs for the year or half-year. This usually takes a series of meetings in which the team members sit around a circle and talk about which topics will be their priorities, who will develop them and what format and timing each will take.

Planning Around a Matrix

Our team has had success in planning around a matrix of five subject areas. After several years of regular brainstorming on what types of programs to offer, we found that our items fell into four and eventually five main categories: spirituality and personal growth, prayer, theology, improving the quality of family life and social justice. We think of these five focus areas as sections of an umbrella under which to plan particular events. Our unwritten rule-of-thumb is to offer two programs or activities under each section during a year's time. (See pages 19-21 for an example of how the matrix was used.)

The focus areas should closely reflect the needs of *your* church community. Of course, they need not be rigidly adhered to in order to be useful. They should serve as guides to keep the planning team from getting stuck in the same general categories year after year. Although variety is important, a team might, occasionally, decide to repeat a successful program, especially if response was enthusiastic and if the team knows that others would like to participate.

A popular speaker, for instance, could be asked to return a year or so later to speak on a different subject.

When the team members reach an agreement on topics, they must also decide which to schedule for the following year and which to schedule long-range. If they want to attract any big-name speakers, they will need calendars for several years ahead. Many top-level speakers book engagements up to three years in advance.

Inviting a speaker—soon or two years from now—is only one way to present a topic. The team now begins to list the possible formats each topic could take. Options are plentiful; they include the following: a demonstration, a film festival, small-group buzz sessions with a facilitator, a retreat based on a theme, an interfaith experience with dialogue, discussion of a taped talk, book discussion with everyone reading the same book, a display of art works on a theme, a shared meal with music, a dramatic production, trips and tours, organized support groups and courses. (Malcolm Knowles extends this list on page 239 of *The Modern Practice of Adult Education*.) It is wise to vary formats if your team offers several events during a season.

After selecting the topics and choosing the formats to present them, the team must decide when to offer them. Give careful consideration to this important issue. It makes a big difference to a parishioner whether "How to Improve a Good Marriage" is offered on Super Bowl Sunday, a weekend evening or a weeknight with babysitting provided. A roundtable discussion on "New Perspectives on Business Ethics" will probably not succeed if offered on a weekday morning when most of the potential attendees are at work. Sensitivity to the rhythms of people's lives is furthered by an atmosphere of frankness among team members as they analyze the possible timing of each event.

Once the topic is selected, the format decided and the proposed timing agreed upon, someone needs to check the parish calendar for any conflicts with other events. Checking in advance on spaces available for the event will avoid a tug-of-war some evening over who has rights to use conference room three.

Finally, the team needs to appoint members who will work out the publicity strategies, get speakers and/or materials and take care of registration and hospitality details.

Example of a One-Year Plan Based on the Five-Section Matrix

Theology

Yahweh, Friend or Foe?	Three lectures by Bob Lawton, S.J.
Post-Apostolic Church	A one-day workshop led by Rev. Raymond Brown, S.S.
Ashes to Easter	A five-week Lenten program based on the lectionary readings. Small group discussion and paraliturgies. Participants meet in homes.
Book Study I and II	Monthly gathering.
What's the Good Word?	Ongoing. Weekly short introductions to the lectionary readings by lay leaders are followed by spirited exchanges by participants in small-group gatherings.
New Possibilities for Parables	A day-long workshop by Mary Boys, Ph.D., on creative use of Scripture.
Our Catholic Roots	A four-part series exploring the origins of Catholic practices such as indulgences and patron saints. Led by Rev. Frank Cancro.

Family Issues

Healing Our Relationships	A series of exercises designed to help people deal with conflicts in relationships. Two evenings led by Mary Thomas Burke, Ph.D.

Seder Supper	Passover celebration followed by a dinner for families. Reservations required.
Creating Family Series	A five-part film series on the challenges and joys of raising children today. Features Clayton Barbeau.

Prayer

***Sadhana* Meditation Group**	An ongoing one-hour meditation group. Some Eastern and Western prayer forms are combined. Meets weekly except summer.
Psalms for Searchers	Three small-group study sessions of how to link psalms with our daily lives. Some journaling and sharing of meditative writing.
Celebrating the Liturgy	Three talks on how the Mass evolved through the ages.
Invitation to Joy	A week of special events for spiritual renewal led by Rev. John Quigley, O.F.M.
Advent: Waiting for the Lord	A day of reflection featuring a film, meditation, shared insights and a simple lunch. Reservations requested.

Social Justice

Peacemaking: Studying the Bishops' Peace Pastoral	Bishop Walter Sullivan, one of the drafters of the Bishops' Peace Pastoral, will share his insights into the scope and purpose of the pastoral.
Christian Unity Week Activities	A week of interdenominational activities built around the theme of seeking unity among Christians. Activities are located at the five participating churches in the area.
Ecumenical Luncheon	A luncheon at First Baptist Church for local clergy and church leaders. Three leaders will be responders to a talk given by Rev. Joseph Champlin on "Working Toward Greater Christian Unity."

Personal Growth

Walking in Gladness: A Course in Healing Life's Hurts	A series of 24 spiritual exercises intended to deepen one's prayer life and help participants get rid of resentments. On audiotape. Developed by Fathers Dennis and Matthew Linn.
Directed Retreat	An eight-day directed retreat of solitude and individual spiritual direction at the Dominican Retreat House in Kingstree, S.C.
Building Better Love Relationships: Friendship and Marriage	Three-part series led by Rev. Frank McNulty.

Checklist

Do you check the parish library for topics and authors that seem in great demand?

Do you contact parish committees and clubs to sound out their program ideas?

Who will review the evaluation sheets at the end of each program?

How do you use evaluation sheets in your planning?

Do you check with the pastor and pastoral staff members to discover any needs they identify in the parish and the community at large?

If you made a survey of needs, how are you using the information?

Do you talk as a team about your own needs for faith development? How does this affect your planning?

Which contemporary (non-Church) issues do your programs touch?

Do you plan a variety of formats for the topics you choose?

Author's Annotated Bibliography

Deboy, James. *Getting Started in Adult Religious Education*. New York: Paulist Press, 1979. Describes goal-setting which can work with the planning process in Chapter Two.

Knowles, Malcolm S. *The Modern Practice of Adult Education*. Chicago: Follett Publishing Company, 1980. A classic manual on adult education. Especially helpful are sections on criteria for selecting board members (p. 77), methods of determining needs (p. 100), recruiting and training leaders and teachers (p. 156) and assessing needs and interests in program planning (pp. 82-118).

Levinson, Daniel J. *The Seasons of a Man's Life*. New York: Alfred A. Knopf, 1978. An exploration of adult growth and development.

McKenzie, Leon. *The Religious Education of Adults*. Birmingham, Ala.: Religious Education Press, 1982. An insightful exploration of adult learning theories with practical tips on program development. Realistic in facing difficulties.

Sheehy, Gail. *Passages*. New York: E.P. Dutton & Company, Inc., 1974. Provocative though somewhat dated book about adult development.

CHAPTER THREE

Publicity—Spreading the Good Word

When I was a learner, I sought both night and day,
I asked the Lord to help me, And He showed me the way.
Go, tell it on the mountain, over the hills and ev'rywhere!
Go, tell it on the mountain, Our Jesus Christ is born.
                                        —Spiritual

The success of an adult faith development program hinges on the team's ability to spread the word about its offerings. Publicity, therefore, plays a key role.

Adult education programs do not command captive audiences as school classes do. Hence, the issue of attracting persons to them becomes primary. When something new is offered, information about it needs to go through a variety of publicity channels to reach as many people as possible—as many times as possible.

Adults with limited time for leisure pursuits will be selective in choosing what they want to learn and the *way* in which their learning will happen. If they come to a program, they will either decide they like it and return, or they will cease to invest their time in such things.

Getting people to come in the first place is the role of the publicist. This team member must catch attention and evoke interest. He or she must also describe the proposed event with clarity and accuracy.

Telling It Often, Telling It Well

Communication experts say that people must hear a message in at least four different ways before it makes an impression. The publicist and team usually have quite a few options from which to choose. Brochures, newspaper articles, paid advertisements, posters, flyers, bulletin announcements, pulpit announcements and telephone chains are among the most popular. Our publicists have found effective ways of using each of these.

Whenever possible we utilize the knowledge of business people on or off the adult faith development team. We look for persons with marketing or media experience who possess expertise in advertising, graphics and copywriting. They are usually pleased to give some time and service in a field of their expertise. They only need an invitation and a specific task.

Writing good copy for brochures or announcements takes special skills. If no professional help is available, ask someone to write copy that answers the five classic journalism questions: Who? What? When? Where? Why? A sixth one to consider at times is "How?" Every newspaper article or piece of advertising copy should address these questions—as we once found by sad experience.

During my first year at the parish, our team planned a series of Sunday afternoon programs during Lent. Everyone wanted the brochure to be special. We spent a considerable amount of money for original artwork for the cover. We secured pictures of all speakers, and we read over and over the copy to make sure the wording was hospitable and energizing. Unfortunately, despite our proofreading, we omitted an important detail—the time of the talks. We ended up with 1,500 beautiful brochures rubberstamped with "All sessions from 3:00 p.m. to 5:00 p.m." We had to order the stamp on overnight service from a local printer. After that, we learned to check and double-check all printed copy with the five W's in mind.

Keeping Costs Down

Printed brochures can be attractive and effective, yet the price of printing can be high. We have found the following ways to cut costs on printing:

Keep the basic design simple. Eliminating pictures, which have to be screen-printed, can save as much as 30 percent on the brochure cost. Colored ink gives your printed piece pizzazz, but it adds considerable cost to the job. Why not consider black ink on a colored paper stock instead? Be sure, however, to consult the printer for the readability of the colored paper. What looks pretty may not provide enough contrast with the ink. A poor combination makes reading difficult, especially for older eyes. Color also can reflect a certain mood. You wouldn't want to use a bright paper stock for a serious or somber program. Your printed pieces should reflect the mood of your program.

Investigate the world of prepress graphics. Typesetting and printing a brochure may not always be necessary. Photocopy businesses will copy a camera-ready pasteup for a fraction of the cost of typesetting. You can include pictures if you have them screen-printed in advance. The cost of the actual screen print is minimal, especially if you are willing to deliver and pick up your own material. Prepress graphics supply borders with gummed backings and even certain types of ready-made artwork to be inserted. Also helpful is graph paper with non-reproducible lines to be used in pasting up material for a flyer or brochure.

Newer word processors and typewriters with automatic margin justification give copy a "printed" look. Some organizations even have headliner machines that offer different styles of type for the title or the major heading. Or you can purchase letters in a variety of styles and sizes to be rubbed off onto the paste-up copy for the headers. You will find many useful materials in commercial art supply stores.

Shop around. Prices can vary as much as $150.00 on an order for 1,500 brochures and most printers will give estimates.

Ask the printer for advice on cost-saving measures. Some

printers are only too glad to share their knowledge with people in church work. Some may even give a church discount. (Always ask!)

Seek out someone with a computer. A team member, or a parishioner willing to help, may have word processing software and the ability to create a brochure or flyer right from the computer screen. If you have access to a laser quality printer with PostScript compatibility, your brochure can have the look of typeset for the mere cost of duplication or photocopying.

Choosing Your Image

The image you create in a brochure is worth careful thought. How can you communicate the content of the program truthfully and make it attractive to the audience you hope to attract? Determine what image you want to create (formal or informal, traditional or progressive, intellectual or emotional and so on). Make sure the person in charge of the brochure is one who can write clear, effective copy and is able to choose the type selection, color and design to achieve the desired image. A brochure printed in Old English script, for example, would not be a good choice for a program geared to an upbeat, contemporary audience.

When you write copy, let your creativity flow from your enthusiasm. Then play with the copy a while before making any final decisions on it. Read the copy aloud to someone. Does it carry the image you want to project? Is it complete? Is it enticing?

Our team sometimes advertises in the newspaper and pays for this from our budget. We advertise when we are having an out-of-town speaker whose message has a fairly wide community appeal. We generally run an advertisement three times—in the Sunday morning paper and a couple of days on either side. In spot-checking people who attend the programs, we have found that some people do come primarily because they have seen the newspaper ad.

Newspaper advertising tends to be expensive. It is not,

however, the only source of newspaper exposure. Local newspapers will accept a well-written news release with those five W's answered. They also will accept items for the community calendar or news tidbits section. Since newspapers vary in their deadline times, a committee person should check out the requirements of different papers and make a list of them.

It helps to get to know the religion editor of your local paper. A personal touch can be effective as you tip them off to your upcoming special events. If you give plenty of advance notice, you will be doing the editor and yourself a favor.

Although bulletin announcements are not the most effective form of publicity, do not overlook them. The bulletin does function as a reminder of upcoming programs. Often people will put a brochure in some safe place and forget to mark their calendars for the events they plan to attend. They will benefit by a reminder close to the event. Of course, church bulletin publicity is limited to members of one church community. If your team has a strong commitment to collaboration, spreading the word beyond the local in-house community is important.

Well-designed posters can draw attention to some events. No one on our team especially likes to make posters, but we found some good sports who are willing to try their hands at one occasionally for a "You-all come" casual event. To give even greater visibility, we purchased a mobile signboard we can place around the church property for different events. We also use it to display library book jackets. The sign is particularly effective when we place it outside the church on Sunday for people to see as they come to Mass.

Oral announcements reach the most people, of course, if they are given at the Sunday Mass. Yet a special spot announcement at parish club meetings can also be quite helpful. Ask a speaker who will be both enthusiastic and specific to plug the event. Before deciding on what to say, the speaker would be wise to ask, "Why would any of these people want to participate in this event?" People will listen to a friendly, clear-talking person who is offering something to enrich their lives. One speaker could go to several organizations or the team can divide up meetings, each member visiting one or two.

Getting on Local TV

Sometimes a local television station will cover an out-of-town speaker. Local talk shows are often hungry for authors or speakers who come to describe their latest project or publication. This generates publicity for both the speaker and the event you are sponsoring. Arrangements are simple to make. Call the station, ask for the talk show host by name and describe to the host the work of the guest speaker. Before you call the station, ask yourself what will be newsworthy about your speaker to people beyond your parish community. Other questions might include:

• Has the speaker experienced the Church in another country or region that would enrich people's understanding of cultural differences?

• Is the speaker involved in a project that is visionary or avant-garde?

• Does the subject matter of the workshop or series of talks meet a significant need for information or support within the community at large?

Making Personal Contacts

We discovered, almost by accident, that telephoning people is worth the time spent in doing it. Two of our daytime classes had small enrollments and we had to decide whether or not to cancel them. A couple of senior citizens volunteered to call parish newcomers who had not received the fall brochure. They made 20 calls. A sufficient number of people responded so that the classes could continue. We experienced a bonus: Those who made the calls were delighted to find that people were grateful to have the information and were glad that someone from the parish was calling them with a personal invitation to come to something. In ministry personal contact is more effective than anything else. John Naisbitt (*Megatrends*) challenges us to more and more personal interaction as our technological society increasingly computerizes information and data about people. He cites evidence of depersonalization in the crowded conditions in cities, the availability of electronic playgrounds in our own homes, computerized banking, personal data banks at doctors' offices and so on. In the midst of this "progress" is an awareness that life is more than functionality.

Our ministry, therefore, needs to be more personal than ever. A highly competitive society prizes rugged individualism and many people have few opportunities for a hospitable encounter. If someone invites you to an event because your presence will contribute to it, the invitation itself is meaningful.

Any government agency or community service committee can offer workshops, but the special quality of a program offered by the Church should be a deep respect for the contribution each person makes simply by being there. Personal contact, though the most time-consuming way of publicizing a program, is the most satisfying to the person invited.

Publicity which happens after the event can be almost as important as spreading the word ahead of time. Bulletin boards which display photographs of past parish events can be a way of increasing interest for future programs. A news report on a speaker's address keeps people alerted to the contemporary nature of the Church's adult offerings.

In the gospels we hear of friends telling other friends that they have found good news. In the first chapter of John's Gospel the disciples literally spread the word ("We have found the Messiah") from person to person. If our efforts to create lively messages about the opportunities for growing in faith are touched by a life-giving encounter with Jesus, our enthusiasm and joy will spill out into these messages.

Checklist

Do you explore getting the most for your publicity money by contacting various printers? What variations in prices do you find?

Do you check each piece of copy for the five W's and make sure that the message is accurate and complete?

Do you use either telephone chains or personal invitations as part of your publicity efforts?

Do you go to various church organizations' meetings to announce events?

Do you use posters, signboards or other visual means to attract the attention of the congregation on Sunday?

Do you contact TV and/or radio stations to arrange an appearance or interview with your speaker?

In what different ways do you publicize each program so that parishioners and others hear the message at least four times?

What image do you convey in both written and spoken announcements for each program?

How do you inform other congregations and community groups about each event?

Author's Annotated Bibliography

Knowles, Malcolm. *The Modern Practice of Adult Education.* Chicago: Follett Publishing Company, 1980. Chapter Nine deals with important information on promotion, preparing printed materials, newspaper publicity and personal contacts.

Shedd, Charlie and Thatcher, Floyd. *Christian Writers Seminar.* Waco, Texas: Creative Resources, 1976. This taped writing program has excellent tips on writing for all kinds of publication, including brochures and posters. It can be ordered by writing to the publisher at 4800 West Waco Dr., Waco, TX 76703.

CHAPTER FOUR

Gaining Support

We spend more on almost any article of bodily aliment or ailment than on our mental aliment. It is time that we had uncommon schools, that we did not leave off our education when we begin to be men and women.

With a little more deliberation in the choice of their pursuits, all men would perhaps become essentially students and observers, for certainly their nature and destiny are interesting to all alike. In accumulating property for ourselves or our posterity, in founding a family or a state, or acquiring fame even, we are mortal; but in dealing with truth we are immortal, and need fear no change nor accident.

—*Henry David Thoreau,* Walden

The adult faith development team may sometimes need to win the support of the pastor and other parish groups.

Many pastors are sincerely grateful for competent people who want to create a special educational ministry to adults. Yet some others are afraid that someone else's programs might not reflect the orthodox teachings of the Church as articulated by the Holy Father. Still others may struggle with the presence of lay persons as partners in ministry.

Certain laypeople may also have difficulty in accepting other lay persons as their leaders in religious education. Like some priests, these parishioners may fear that the leaders will not be orthodox enough for them. Others will say that they learned their religion by going to a Catholic school in childhood and that they have no need for further education—and see no need for funds for adult education and faith development.

When a pastor and/or parishioners do feel uneasy about an adult education lay coordinator and team, the team must begin the process of gaining trust. In some cases, this may take a long time. Frankly it may sometimes even be impossible to create the kind of healthy climate necessary to nurture faith. In most situations, however, some knowledge and some trust-building skills can facilitate a change of attitudes.

Arm Yourself With Church Documents

Begin by becoming familiar with what the Church documents say about the ministry of adult faith development. An important one is *Sharing the Light of Faith: The National Catechetical Directory for Catholics of the U.S.*, published in 1979 by the U.S. Catholic Conference, Department of Education. In this small, clearly written book the bishops emphasize the importance of programs for adults. The following quotations are from Chapter Eight, "Catechesis Toward Maturity in Faith":

> The act of faith is a free response to God's grace; and maximum human freedom only comes with the self-possession and responsibility of adulthood. This is one of the principal reasons for regarding adult catechesis as the chief form of catechesis. To assign primacy to adult catechesis does not mean sacrificing catechesis at other age levels; it means making sure that what is done earlier is carried to its culmination in adulthood. (Sec. 188)
>
> Because of its importance and because all other forms of catechesis are oriented in some way to it, the catechesis of adults must have high priority at all levels of the Church. The success of programs for children and youth depends to a significant extent upon the words, attitudes, and actions of the adult community, especially parents, family, and guardians.(Sec. 188)

To Teach as Jesus Did is another document which sets

direction for adult learning in the Church. The U.S. Catholic Conference published it in 1972. This passage deals with the specific task of educational ministry to adults:

Today, perhaps more than ever before, it is important to recognize that learning is a lifelong experience. Rapid, radical changes in contemporary society demand well-planned, continuing efforts to assimilate new data, new insights, new modes of thinking and acting. This is necessary for adults to function efficiently, but, more important, to achieve full realization of their potential as persons whose destiny includes but also transcends this life. Thus, they will also enjoy ever-deepening fellowship within the many communities to which each of them belongs. Consequently, the continuing education of adults is situated not at the periphery of the Church's educational mission but at its center. (#43)
It is essential that such programs recognize not only the particular needs of adults, but also their maturity and experience. Those who teach in the name of the Church do not simply instruct adults, but also learn from them; they will only be heard by adults if they listen to them. For this reason, adult programs must be planned and conducted in ways that emphasize self-direction, dialogue, and mutual responsibility. (#44)

Know You Are *Called and Gifted*

In 1980 on the occasion of the 15th anniversary of Vatican II's *Decree on the Apostolate of Lay People*, the National Council of Catholic Bishops issued another document, *Called and Gifted*. The following statement from it stresses the importance of the parish in responding to adult religious growth needs.

The Second Vatican Council clearly proclaimed the universal call to holiness. Not only are lay people included in God's call to holiness, but theirs is a unique call requiring a unique response which itself is a gift of the Holy Spirit. It is characteristic that lay men and women hear the call to holiness in the very web of their

35

existence (*Lumen Gentium* #31), in and through the events of the world, the pluralism of modern living, the complex decisions and conflicting values they must struggle with, the richness and fragility of sexual relationships, the delicate balance between activity and stillness, presence and privacy, love and loss. (#12)

The response of lay people to this call promises to contribute still more to the spiritual heritage of the Church. Already the laity's hunger for God's word is everywhere evident. Increasingly, lay men and women are seeking spiritual formation and direction in deep ways of prayer. This has helped to spur several renewal movements. (#13)

These developments present a challenge to the parish because, for the most part, the spiritual needs of lay people must be met in the parish. The parish must be a home where they can come together with their leaders for mutual spiritual enrichment, much as in the early Church: "They devoted themselves to the apostles' instruction and the communal life, to the breaking of bread and the prayers" (Acts 2:42). (#14)

The *Decree on the Apostolate of Lay People*, as well as the other documents of Vatican II, provides a wealth of inspiration and information. It clearly mandates that lay persons and priests work together in close association. It encourages laypeople to bring their experience of living in contemporary society to influence pastoral leadership. It calls for dialogue between priests and laypeople as a means of resolving questions of the world and of salvation.

> Participators in the function of Christ, priest, prophet and king, the laity have an active part of their own in the life and action of the Church. Their action within the Church communities is so necessary that without it the apostolate of the pastors will frequently be unable to obtain its full effect....
>
> The parish offers an outstanding example of community apostolate, for it gathers into a unity all the human diversities that are found there and inserts them into the universality of the Church. The laity should develop the habit of working in the parish in close union with their priests, of bringing before the ecclesial community their own problems, world

problems, and questions regarding man's salvation, to examine them together and solve them by general discussion. (#10)

The process of gathering adults into small communities for support and discussion finds strong encouragement in this same document:

> The individual apostolate has a special field in regions where Catholics are few and scattered. In such circumstances the laity who exercise only the personal apostolate...can gather for discussion into small groups with no rigid form of rules or organization. This is particularly appropriate in the present instance, for it ensures the continual presence before the eyes of others of a sign of the Church's community, a sign that will be seen as a genuine witness of love. Thus, by affording mutual spiritual aid by friendship and the exchange of personal experiences, they get the courage to surmount the difficulties of too isolated a life and activity and can increase the yield of their apostolate. (#17)

In the eyes of the Council Fathers, not even the circumstance of living in a rural environment without the benefit of an organized pastorate excuses the Christian from the important work of gathering with other Christians to discuss and share their lived experience of faith.

Be Encouraged by Leadership Support

Even more encouraging is the statement from the *Decree on the Apostolate of Lay People* which indicates how the involvement of the laity in the ministry of the Church is to be received:

> Pastors are to welcome these lay persons with joy and gratitude. They will see to it that their conditions of life satisfies as perfectly as possible the requirements of justice, equity and charity, chiefly in the matter of resources necessary for the maintenance of themselves

and their families. They should too be provided with the necessary training and with spiritual comfort and encouragement. (#22)

Chapter Five of the Decree, "The Preservation of Good Order," calls for ongoing adult education and recommends solid instruction in theology, ethics, philosophy and general culture.

Instruction in human relations is also greatly encouraged, "especially the art of living and working on friendly terms with others and entering into dialogue with them" (Chapter Six, #29).

Further emphasis is placed on education and training for the apostolate as ongoing:

> Inasmuch as the human person is continuously developing and new problems are forever arising, this education should be steadily perfected; it requires an ever more thorough knowledge and a continual adaptation of action. While meeting all its demands, concern for the unity and integrity of the human person must be kept always in the foreground, in order to preserve and intensify its harmony and equilibrium. (#29)

The conclusion of Chapter Six encourages the use of many resources in adult faith development:

> Many aids are now at the disposal of the laity who devote themselves to the apostolate: namely, sessions, congresses, recollections, retreats, frequent meetings, conferences, books and periodicals; all these enable them to deepen their knowledge of holy scripture and Catholic doctrine, nourish the spiritual life, and become acquainted also with world conditions and discover and adopt suitable methods.
>
> These educational aids take into account the various types of apostolate exercised in this or that particular area.
>
> With this end in view higher centers or institutes have been created; these have already given excellent results.
>
> The Council rejoices at initiatives of this kind now

flourishing in certain regions; it desires to see them take root in other places too, wherever the need for them makes itself felt.

Moreover, centers of documentation and research should be established, not only in theology but also in anthropology, psychology, sociology, methodology, for the benefit of all fields of the apostolate. The purpose of such centers is to create a more favorable atmosphere for developing the aptitudes of the laity, men and women, young and old. (#32)

I have quoted from these documents at length because few people realize the extraordinary support which the Church offers for ministry to and by adults. Statements by both the Vatican and the American bishops encourage laypeople to minister in faith development on every level. They encourage parishes and dioceses to budget adequately for it, to seek cooperative ways for priest and people to work together, to adapt teaching techniques to age and cultural differences, to value whatever fosters human relations. These statements encourage dioceses to expand the development of institutes and resources in the study of anthropology, psychology, sociology and methodology for the development of all persons in the Church. Knowing the documents and letting others know what the Church has said is one way to build support for an emerging adult faith development program.

Spread the Good Words Around

How can we spread the good news of these encouraging documents on the parish level? One way is to include short quotations from them in reports and memos as inspirational reminders of the mission at hand. Another is to weave them into a major presentation which could be given at a parish council or education commission meeting. I have put quotations from these documents on a set of transparencies and used them to illustrate a talk on why adult faith development needs attention in the parish today.

Parish groups are often eager to find someone to present such a program—and an in-parish speaker is easy on the program budget.

In addition to publicizing Church documents, an effective adult educator will let people know that the input they give through questionnaires, focus groups and evaluations is being used in planning. If you thank groups periodically for their financial support, their attendance and their ideas, you will create a climate of positive regard for your ministry. Parishioners—even those not able to participate—will gradually realize that successful programs are the successes of their entire parish. A wise team looks for continual opportunities to give brief updates on educational happenings. Send written and personal reports of successes and coming events to committees just to keep channels open.

A pastor's endorsement usually boosts the image of adult education offerings. We regularly reserve a space on our brochures for the pastor's message of encouragement. Most pastors are willing to do this.

Record and Report

Accountability and carefully kept financial records also strengthen parishioners' trust. Donors need to know that their contributions at a parish mission, for example, actually go to the cause for which they gave the money. Parish adult education leaders should do all they can to build a climate of trust by managing money responsibly and by offering financial updates periodically.

Gaining support and trust takes continual effort, especially in keeping everyone informed. But the results are worth the effort. Cooperation of priests, people and parish leaders makes the ministry of planning for adults enjoyable and more effective.

Checklist

Which statements of the Vatican II Council on Education have you read?

Have you familiarized yourselves with *The National Catechetical Directory*?

Who has read *To Teach as Jesus Did* and *Called and Gifted*?

Do your reports and presentations include quotes from the major statements on adult education in the Church?

Does your pastor write endorsements of your programs for your publicity?

Do you keep careful financial records?

Author's Annotated Bibliography

Flannery, Austin, O.P., ed. *Vatican II: The Conciliar and Post-Conciliar Documents*. Northport, N.Y.: Costello Publishing Co., Inc., 1987.

National Conference of Catholic Bishops. *Sharing the Light of Faith*. Washington, D.C.: U.S. Catholic Conference, 1979.

National Conference of Catholic Bishops. *To Teach as Jesus Did*. Washington, D.C.: U.S. Catholic Conference, 1973.

National Conference of Catholic Bishops. *Called and Gifted: The American Catholic Laity*. Washington, D.C.: U.S. Catholic Conference, 1980.

Hospitality—More Than Punch and Cookies

Let mutual love continue. Do not neglect hospitality, for through it some have unknowingly entertained angels.

—*Hebrews 13:1—2*

When participants talk about their good experiences at adult education gatherings, they often hint of receiving something intangible and difficult to put into words. Some say, "I liked the friendliness of the group." Others comment that they felt at home; they were surprised to find other people with the same questions and problems. These remarks about friendliness and belonging challenge a planning team to take a new look at the importance of hospitality. How do we help create a climate where adults feel at home so that they can be invited to share their faith journeys with others?

My husband and I introduced our children to the social life of preschool with a book by Miriam Cohen called *Will I Have A Friend?* It deals with the anxiety a child feels about approaching that first experience at school. Actually, the book tackles a basic fear for people of *all* ages—one we feel as we consider whether or not to attend a parish gathering: Will anyone there talk to me and be friendly? Some persons miss wonderful opportunities because they fear feeling alone or out of place.

Much hidden work goes into making programs hospitable. Participants will feel more welcome if the team plans the details of hospitality so as to focus attention on the guests. The committee needs to decide who will provide a welcoming handshake, distribute printed materials, provide nametags and point out the restrooms. Although nametags help people identify one another, aware team members can make conversation easier by introducing persons to each other. Besides planning when to plug in the coffee pot (Don't forget, large pots can take up to 45 minutes to perk!), the team should discuss who will preside at the refreshment table and select a person whose friendly personality invites chatting during break time. Home-baked cookies on a tray and a responsive person serving them speak clearly of warmth and welcome. Offering food and drink with friendliness during breaks is an excellent way to help people feel at home.

Child care frees parents to participate in adult education events. Arranging for babysitting takes time, but it is a way of saying, "We want to do all we can to encourage you to come." I have heard young parents comment that they could not have attended a parish retreat, for instance, if child care had not been offered. Teams handle the babysitting arrangements in various ways. Some ask parents to reserve a place for their child by calling the parish office a few days ahead of time. This helps the team know how many sitters to engage. Others ask youth groups to take on babysitting as a project and ask them to manage the details.

Decide who will introduce the program and preside. The presider should get some biographical information on a speaker and give an overview of the session. The presider might want to recommend materials from the church library as a follow-up or mention a related program from another church at the end of the session. The person presiding should thank the participants warmly and recognize the encouragement their presence gives to others in the parish.

Invite Hospitable Speakers

Speakers themselves create an accepting climate—or hinder it. Before deciding to invite a particular speaker, check out the following questions:

• What is the model of communication he or she uses? In transactional analysis terms, is it adult/adult or parent/child?

• Is the presenter able to be influenced by the comments of the participants, or does the speaker have to "answer" every remark as an ultimate authority?

• Does the speaker welcome interaction or see it as an interruption of the topic to be covered?

Pedantic put-downs such as "You see?" and "What I'm trying to make clear to you..." offend adult participants. Planners need to be sensitive to the effect patronizing attitudes will have on a group so that they choose teachers and facilitators who respect other adults as equals. Leaders need to come more as fellow journeyers and less as experts. Such leaders invite adults to talk about their own insights more freely.

Arrange chairs to create a welcoming space for people to spend time with each other. Immovable chairs or church pews are, undeniably, the least hospitable offerings for adult posteriors. Besides, people who cannot see each other cannot interact well—verbally or nonverbally. Equally unfriendly are third-grade desks sometimes offered at sacramental preparation programs for parents. The room should have comfortable chairs that can be moved into all kinds of arrangements that enhance participation. Attractive, comfortable adult chairs may be expensive. An environment speaks, however, and it should assure adults that they belong there.

Observing the time frame stated in the publicity materials helps to create a comfortable environment. That means all equipment, tables, exhibits and refreshment areas need to be set up well in advance of the time advertised as the beginning of the session. Be generous in allowing set-up time. Our team found that, despite careful planning, the "unexpected" often happened moments before people arrived. If someone misplaces the insides to the coffee pot or forgets to pack the power cord for the overhead projector, the team will still have time to remedy the situation if they have started early. As people arrive, team members should relax and greet them. The messy details of set-up should be over by this time.

Sessions also need to end on time. Occasionally a speaker may get wrapped up in an issue that cannot be left dangling, but most speakers who contract for a two-hour presentation want to get going at the end of the second hour. If questions from the audience are part of the program, allow a designated period of time for this and let the presenter know in advance. Don't expect the speaker to hang around for an extra half-hour to handle questions.

Participants should not have to tiptoe awkwardly toward the exit because a session goes well beyond the stated ending time. If a speaker wants to extend the evening for a few who want to continue talking, the team should announce the extension for those who want to stay and gracefully release those who are not interested or who have babysitters and therefore must get home.

Usually team members do not have much control over parking arrangements. They can make sure, however, that clear signs direct participants from the parking lot to the meeting place. Teams often assume parishioners know the location of the conference rooms. But parish halls can be a bewildering maze to newcomers. A wise team makes people comfortable by providing signs or printing a small map in publicity materials.

If smoking is allowed, someone needs to designate which areas are for smokers and set out ashtrays. Smokers, especially, might need frequent breaks. Don't forget to let the speaker know ahead of time when you want to schedule a brief break and to ask the speaker about smoking preferences. If a team decides not to allow smoking, try to get the message across in a friendly way. Moralizing about the offensiveness of smoking doesn't win friends or create a welcoming atmosphere.

Consider Carefully Location and Time

Do consider the accessibility of your location for persons with disabilities. If ramps are not available, the team could designate someone to assist persons in wheelchairs to negotiate any difficult areas. A person in a wheelchair can find even a small step a major obstacle, especially in bad weather.

Most churches have restrooms which accommodate wheelchairs, but if yours does not, the adult education team might try gently persuading the finance committee to provide one.

The scheduling of programs needs to be accommodating. The natural rhythms of people's lives suggest that programs geared to the majority of parish members be saved for times other than Super Bowl Sunday or graduation week. Parish teams need to be aware if most people in their town go to the Tuesday evening basketball games. By thinking through these issues, the parish team can extend invitations to their programs which will be considered.

Adults come to programs with a gamut of needs. Some seek information; others need to vent frustration. Many look for companionship. A few show up because they have been asked to help and feel a stake in the process. All need to know that they are in a psychologically safe environment, one where their own experiences of living will be respected and valued. They must feel secure enough to pose their own questions and know that none is too basic or foolish to ask. They need assurance, also, that their questioning adds vitality to their faith journey and that answers will unfold in moments of reflection upon the movement of their own lives. They need to hear that the very process of wrestling with an issue—when shared with others—becomes an important step in the faith journey of other people, too.

To a beginning team, attention to the details of hospitality might seem like a frill, something to do if there's extra time. Helping people feel at home and cared for, however, is central to gathering any group for adult faith development. We can't answer ultimate questions which bring us face-to-face with mystery. But we can create a safe "home" environment which protects and nourishes the freedom to explore such questions. As Mary and Martha of Bethany provided a haven of safety and hospitality for Jesus, adult educators reach out in the same way.

Punch and cookies and a hospitable environment do not guarantee success in adult education programs. When they are signs, however, of that deeper openness which makes true human encounter possible, they become the "sacramentals" of a new kind of community, one in which "Night will be no more, nor will they need light from lamp or sun, for the Lord God shall give them light, and they shall reign forever and ever" (Revelation 22:5).

Checklist

Do the sessions begin and end on time so that people are not inconvenienced?

Is the scheduling hospitable for adults? Does it consider the natural rhythms of people's lives and avoid times like Super Bowl Sunday and graduation week?

Do you set up audiovisual equipment and the hospitality table before people arrive so the planning team can greet people and mingle?

Are the facilities comfortable, clean and climate-controlled?

Are the restrooms conveniently located and fully equipped?

Is someone prepared to talk with people or to recommend resources such as books and community groups as follow-up?

Do you affirm participants and thank them for their supportive presence?

Do you provide babysitting?

Do the arrangement of chairs and the room offer hospitable space for interaction with others?

Do your speakers convey respect and positive regard for their audiences?

Author's Annotated Bibliography

Girzaitis, Loretta. *The Church as Reflecting Community*. West Mystic, Conn.: Twenty-Third Publications, 1977. Chapter on "Community as Educator" reflects the importance of a welcoming community. Good suggestions for how large parishes can break down the anonymity that tempts people to believe they are unimportant to the mission of the Church.

Knowles, Malcolm. *The Modern Practice of Adult Education*. Chicago: The Follett Publishing Company, 1980. Chapter Eleven discusses the importance of setting a climate for learning. See also Chapter Four, "Self-Concepts and Teachers' Concepts of Learners."

Nouwen, Henri. *Reaching Out*. Garden City, N.Y.: Doubleday and Company, Inc., 1975. Chapter Four discusses the nature of hospitality to strangers. Chapter Five explores forms of hospitality.

CHAPTER SIX

The Care and Feeding of Speakers

Whoever has received knowledge
and eloquence in speech from God
should not be silent or secretive
but demonstrate it willingly.
When a great good is widely heard of,
then, and only then, does it bloom,
and when that good is praised by [people],
it has spread its blossoms.
　　　—*Marie de France,* The Lais of Marie de France

What is pleasanter than the tie of host and guest?"
　　　—*Aeschylus,* The Libation Bearers

People take their seats in a semicircular arrangement as conversation begins to wane, then softens to silence. Someone walks briskly to the podium to introduce a priest from New Jersey named Father Frank McNulty and a talk called "What's for Dinner."

This moment has not come about effortlessly. Many people have brought it about by working together behind the scenes. Someone has suggested the speaker and topic and talked about whether that person would be able to communicate in language people can understand. Someone contacted him and negotiated the fee for his talk. Another picked him up at the airport. Others arranged for his meals and, most importantly, showed him warmth and courtesy.

51

Hospitality to the speaker can make a difference in the quality of the program. Whether speakers offer a string of academic degrees or life experiences as credentials, they all welcome relaxation and friendliness from us so that they can create a hospitable climate for learning and sharing.

If your speaker is from out of town, the team begins a warmer relationship when one or two members meet the speaker at the airport and take him or her to the place of lodging. The team is responsibile to provide for the lodging and meals. You can invite the speaker to stay in someone's home or at a local hotel—at the parish's expense, of course. If the priests of your parish invite a priest-speaker to stay at their rectory, make sure that you know what happens at meals. Rectory mealtimes can be chaotic and unplanned. If they are, invite the priest to someone's home or to a restaurant for dinner with you. Give your guest a caring and comfortable time in your city.

Be aware that your guest might want a good night's sleep to prepare for your event. It is wise to ask openly when they prefer to return alone to their rooms.

As another way of offering hospitality to out-of-town and local speakers, teams can invite the speakers to an "unwinding" get-together after the event. Be sure, however, to give your speakers the option of leaving easily whenever they might want to. Most speakers like feedback or, at least, some friendly company to help process the talk, consider questions which were raised and evaluate the interaction which was stimulated. The speaker and a group may go out to a restaurant afterwards or meet at someone's home. Most of our speakers have expressed gratitude for this kind of gathering. Our team also finds this a wonderful way to relax and process the evening.

A letter of thanks to every speaker is the final gesture of hospitality. Some adult coordinators feel that if an honorarium is given, an additional letter of thanks is not needed. Most speakers, however, put forth extra effort to prepare fine presentations and be available for questions and personal interaction as well. Very few whom we have invited have even specified a set fee, preferring instead to take whatever honorarium is offered. Unfortunately most honorariums offered to speakers on religious topics are not comparable to those offered in the professional and business world. A letter of thanks helps to express gratitude and to create goodwill. I have been pleasantly surprised, too, at the number of speakers who also write to thank us for inviting them and for the hospitality they received.

Part of the team's hospitality is setting a pace for the program by providing a brief introduction for the speaker. When a speaker agrees to come, a team member should ask for a vita giving the speaker's academic, professional and personal achievements. The introduction should contain some of this information, especially why he or she is qualified to talk on the subject at hand. Most audiences also appreciate knowing something personal and human about the person before them.

The introduction should always be prepared ahead of time. Avoid putting the speaker in an awkward position a few minutes before the talk with, "What do you want me to say about you?"

If different team members introduce different speakers, parishioners will also get to know some of the persons who have worked so hard behind the scenes. Different team members also offer a variety of styles of introduction.

Make sure that the speaker's table has water or coffee and check with the speaker for beverage preferences. Be sure that the microphone is in working order and at an appropriate height.

Another item of information to find out in advance is whether the speaker has published any books or articles which might be made available for sale to the audience. Occasionally a magazine will offer reprints of articles if they have advance notice. Some publishers will send books on consignment for an author's appearance and some also offer a special reduction for bulk orders. Be sure to allow plenty of time, six weeks or so, for your books to arrive. In an emergency, publishers can get books to you by air freight on 24-hour notice, but the expense can be high.

Be sure to give local speakers clear directions or send a map that also identifies places to park and the entrance to use. A team member should always look out for the presenter's arrival to offer welcome, help carry any materials or set up visuals.

Checklist

Do you plan the speaker's meals before and after the presentation?

Do you talk with the speaker about the topic and the audience the topic was likely to attract?

Do you:

1) take care of chalkboard and flip charts?

2) prepare a glass of water for each speaker to have during the presentation?

3) check the condition of the media equipment?

4) plan the seating for small-group interaction?

5) provide name tags?

Do you plan who will welcome the people?

Do you have books, articles or tapes authored by your speaker on hand for participants?

Do you write a letter of appreciation, thanking the speaker for his or her work?

Author's Annotated Bibliography

Knowles, Malcolm. *The Modern Practice of Adult Education.* Chicago: The Follett Publishing Company, 1980. Pages 156 to 159 deal with the difficult subject of how much compensation to give workshop leaders and lecturers and how to recruit good ones.

McKenzie, Leon. *The Religious Education of Adults.* Birmingham, Ala.: Religious Education Press, 1982. Chapter Eight, "Teaching: An Analysis," contains invaluable suggestions for the hiring of workshop presenters and speakers.

CHAPTER SEVEN

Using Films and Videotapes Effectively

One picture is worth a thousand words.

—Old adage

When Marshall McLuhan called the world of the 1960's to recognize that "the medium is the message," educators had already been using films, filmstrips and television regularly for many years. They were, however, just beginning to take advantage of videocassettes.

Since that time, the number of top-level religious educators which we can invite into our parish halls through video programs has multiplied with amoebic rapidity. We can find lively, engaging videos on basic Catholic teaching, family spirituality, sacramental preparation, liturgy, moral theology, prayer and Scripture interpretation. (See the list of catalogs of various religious publishing companies in the resource guide on pages 85-92.)

Film and video can help provide excellent programs even on a limited budget. Successful use of these visuals, however, requires more from the team than arranging for a notice in the church bulletin and flipping the play button on the designated evening. Team members must preview the film, prepare materials and provide persons to facilitate interaction in the follow-up time. If you want a memorable and educationally profitable evening, you will also provide the same services as you would for any other program— publicity, hospitality, a sense of community and so on.

Previewing a film well in advance is essential. By doing

so you will be able to prepare adequately for the discussion. You will anticipate questions and problems that may arise. You may even decide that this film will not be as helpful as you thought—that you might like a substitute. (Or you may discover—in time—that you received the wrong film through a shipping error.) If the team members have an understanding of the film's message and the way it is presented, they will feel the kind of professional confidence that helps to provide a smoothly run and stimulating program.

Read guidesheets that come with the film or videotape well ahead of time also. Some will offer suggestions for further reading and follow-up activities. For example, the Franciscan Communications program, *Creating Family*, provides questions for people to take home and use in family discussions. Others offer creative ideas, activities or group discussion. You may wish to type or photocopy some of these. (For copyrighted materials you will have to write the publishers for permission to photocopy or reprint.) You may wish to develop your own questions or ways of responding to the film. Long before your program, be sure to reproduce the materials you want to distribute for reflection or discussion. Copy machines have a reputation for breaking down half an hour before a program.

Remember also that an equipment failure can destroy a program based on a film or video. Try this preventive practice: Imagine the worst that can happen. You will then check all of your equipment and the quality of your reception. You will make sure you have adapters, extra exciter lamps, extension cords taped to the floor and so on. You will insert the film or video, set it at its beginning (skipping ads, previews and so on), adjust focus and regulate volume. Make sure, also, that seats are arranged for a full view of the screen. Attention to details ahead of time insures a smoothly run program and avoids the audience restlessness that results from waiting, watching visual adjustments and listening to blaring patches of sound being leveled.

Planning Your Program

You might want to create a warm and open atmosphere by beginning the program with a prayer service which has songs or Scripture passages carrying the same theme as the film. People also feel a sense of community when they can sing together and move together into the spirit of the presentation.

Discussion guides usually offer suggestions for group interaction after the film, but you may still want to develop your own questions to evoke the type of sharing you want. Questions designed to elicit information are usually confined to the action and characters of the film itself. Information-seeking questions are nonthreatening and encourage people to begin talking aloud. They make safe openers. Some types of questions invite people to compare their experiences to those of the film characters. This kind of sharing frequently helps develop bonds among group members.

Jacques Weber, a veteran adult educator and lecturer, reminds his hearers, "Adults learn what they want to, when they want to, and in the way they want to." Adults learn best when they can think and talk about their own life journeys in relationship to a stimulus such as a film. You can design your questions to bring this about. For example, try asking, "When have you experienced a struggle like *(person in film)*?" or "What memories of your joy-full experiences of Church does *(situation in film)* evoke?" Tap the resource of the participant's experience of living.

Plan in some detail the group interaction after the film. Will you ask the participants to stay as one group or break into small groups? If small groups, how will they be formed? By participants' choices? By assigning numbers? Do you want to ask team members or others ahead of time to be group leaders? Or ask each small group to select its own leader? Or ask all members of the group to be equally responsible for the discussion? Do the groups or group leaders need any guidelines? Will you give these verbally or in printed form? If you need help in making wise decisions about group interaction, consult your local librarian for books and resources about group dynamics and group leadership.

Allow enough time for people to enhance their friendships in the community. People like to chat informally as well as in their structured discussions.

If your parish has a bookrack, library or resource center, select books and tapes to have on hand. You will be offering interested participants an opportunity to continue to learn or to follow up on their insights and inspirations. When we showed Clayton Barbeau's *How to Raise Parents*, for instance, we arranged a table with books that included James DiGiacomo's *We Were Never Their Age*, tapes such as John Powell's *The Growing Edge of Life* and Joseph Champlin's pamphlet "Roots, Wings and Embraces."

In deciding your time frame, allow for all the evening's activities. The introduction to the film, a refreshment break, the time it takes to get in—and out of—small groups, the introduction of extra resources and any follow-up activities all carry a certain price tag of time.

Videos are quite adaptable for small groups. For example, you might minister to people who have suffered a recent loss by inviting them to films such as *Minnie Remembers*, *My Garden* or *Harriet*. For parents—or young adults—you might plan one or more of Mass Media Ministries' short films (under 30 minutes) on television advertising. Some of them include *The 30-Second Dream*, *Marketing the Myths* and *Television, the Enchanted Mirror*. Larger groups can be accommodated by 16mm film if you have a fairly large screen.

Film and videotape offer some unique possibilities for publicity. If you are using a film with imaginative characters and if you can find a good sport to volunteer, why not have a character from one of the films "visit" parish groups to tell them of the coming event?

Outside of your regular programs, you can use video in other creative ways for adult faith development. Some teams offer to lead the opening prayer for parish organizations and do so with short meditative films followed by a few minutes of reflection from the members. Participants enter into each other's faith life and this kind of prayer sets a positive tone for a meeting.

Good film and video programs are worth the time they take. You can check out the ever-expanding titles available by perusing some catalogs such as those listed in the Resource Guide.

Checklist

Do you check out the equipment, room arrangement and lighting ahead of time?

Do you preview the film and discussion guide in order to suggest follow-up reading or future programs?

Do you prepare your facilitators with synopses of the films or with sample discussion questions?

Do you allow ample time for informal conversation?

Do your questions encourage people to talk about their own experiences and faith rather than to repeat content from a film?

Do some of your programs meet the needs of small groups or marginal groups?

Do you design some innovative publicity for any program?

Author's Annotated Bibliography

Armsey, James W. and Dahl, Norman C. *An Inquiry Into the Uses of Instructional Technology.* New York: The Ford Foundation, 1973. Examines trends and practical application of media options.

Knowles, Malcolm. *The Modern Practice of Adult Education.* Chicago: Follett Publishing Company, 1980. Pages 134 and 135 cover briefly the option of using videotaped materials for programs.

Rossi, Peter and Biddle, Bowe, eds. *The New Media and Education*. Chicago: Aldine Publishing Company, 1966. Describes some new options available in educational methods due to technological developments.

CHAPTER EIGHT

Choosing Criteria for Success

[D]o not depend on the hope of results. When you are doing the sort of work you have taken on, essentially an apostolic work, you may have to face the fact that your work will be apparently worthless and even achieve no results at all, if not perhaps results apposite to what you expect. As you get used to this idea, you start more and more to concentrate not on the results but on the value, the rightness, the truth of the work itself. And there too a great deal has to be gone through, as gradually you struggle less and less for an idea and more and more for specific people. The range tends to narrow down, but it gets much more real. In the end . . . it is the reality of personal relationships that saves everything.
—Thomas Merton, "Letter to a Young Activist."

"How many people showed up?" is all too often the first question people ask after a program. Directors frequently feel defensive about the number they give (no matter what it is)—sensing that "success equals big crowds" for the person asking. Who measures success? By what criteria?

We need to determine success or failure in the light of our immediate goal for a particular program and of our visions for the future.

In an earlier chapter, we spoke of the need to plan overall goals for the year. For example, if, as a general goal, the team decides to start Bible sharing groups, a way of evaluating how effectively this goal was met would be to poll the participants and ask for feedback on their experience. Even participants who came for a short time and then dropped out should be contacted because their insights can often help improve a program.

Each individual program should have its own goal— one that keeps in mind the year's goals. The evaluation sheet should carry specific questions to help the team know if the goal has been met. (See Appendix A on page 83 for a sample evaluation form.) For instance, a program for parents of children enrolled in Sunday religious education classes might aim to foster a spirit of community among these parents. The evaluation sheet could ask questions like: Did you meet any other parents as a result of this program? Did you share any opinions, questions or information with others? Did anyone share any ideas with you?

If a team decides that one goal will be to attract business people, then an evaluation should include such questions as "Were the program hours convenient for your work schedule?" and "Did the program address any issues you face in your work environment?"

Evaluation based on these goals is essential. The team needs to set aside time regularly to discuss the evaluative data. Notes should be taken at this meeting so they can be used in planning future programs.

Consider *all* your sources of evaluation. Your feedback sheets have the highest value. But team members attending the program may get more nuanced opinions from talking to the participants. Team members also bring their own perceptions of how people received the program, of the degree of sharing, sense of community building and so on. Checking with the pastoral staff often brings in more information.

Evaluating a program begins with asking if the goal of the program was fulfilled—and to what degree. The team will usually feel relaxed and comfortable if the answer is positive. But what if it is not? What if evaluation sheets are discouragingly negative—confirming what the attending team members felt all along?

The team asks: Why wasn't the goal met? The answer may be obvious: A power failure set the program back 30 minutes and people were restless; the weather was not conducive to travel; the speaker droned on in a monotone. The answer may be more subtle: Was the speaker talking over the heads of people? Was the speaker too simple, underestimating the background of the audience? Were the facilitators insufficiently skilled for difficulties which arose? Was the choice of topic out of sync with people's interests? Did publicity reach the target audience?

For planning purposes, members need to accept a failure and honestly face the reasons for it. When a goal isn't met, team members can be tempted to discouragement—a real enemy of ministry. Discouragement needs to be met with creativity, reason and hope.

Any program can be an opportunity to learn something. What may be a failure in terms of immediate goals may be a success in some other way. Discouragement is overcome by counting and rejoicing in each success.

Jesuit psychologist John Powell says, "Your vision determines your values." We can apply that phrase as we evaluate both successful programs and ones that seemed to fail. We need a broad vision of the benefits of adult programs to help us evaluate effectively. Here are some questions to help clarify your vision.

Did the event minister to a group that often feels left out of the mainstream of parish potlucks and clubs?

Occasionally planners will become so family-oriented that they forget to offer programs for groups such as singles or those coping with divorce. With a perhaps misplaced enthusiasm for large crowds, teams can easily overlook the needs of smaller groups such as the disabled, refugees and the unemployed. We can be oblivious to those whose life situations call for a program geared to their special circumstances—simply because they are fewer in number.

Our team discovered this one summer when we ran the Argus *Fully Alive Experience*, a 10-week program aimed at personal psychospiritual growth. We advertised the series for couples and singles without giving much consideration to the wording. Of the 15 people who rang our doorbell the first night, 11 were single, divorced or widowed. Many were experiencing painful emotional struggles. They expressed gratitude for a church program geared to their personal growth. They were tired of feeling like they were being treated as second-rate Catholics because they couldn't claim a spouse and a family of five kids. We noted the wonderful supportive community which these people formed. It led to a significant experience of Church for all of us. With a vision of community building and individual growth in mind, we counted this program a wonderful success.

Did the program build ecumenical or inter-parish cooperation? Consider a program successful if new bridges are built that can be crossed over and over again in the future.

Attendance is often small at inter-parish events since many parishioners are reluctant to venture across town—or even across parish boundaries—to attend a new program. But cooperative relationships usually lead to growth, and word-of-mouth news about interesting programs will increase the number attending eventually—despite distance.

Two parishes near us cooperated in presenting a series on the bishops' peace pastoral. Of 1,500 possible participants, only 10 showed. While the event appeared to be a failure in terms of numbers, it turned out to be the first of several co-sponsored projects. Preparing the program developed cooperation between parishes which had never worked together effectively.

Was the level of participation in the program high? Were there many questions, comments and much energetic interaction among the participants?

A basic principle of education at any level is that learning increases with the degree of the learner's involvement. While a spellbinding speaker may draw big crowds, a lecture is not the most effective way to learn. Rev. Kevin Coughlin, author of *Motivating Adults for Religious Education*, claims that the lecture series is actually the least effective kind of program because it leaves little time for exploring life-experiences—a process so important for religious growth. In our parish, although we have offered lecture series which drew 200 people, we rejoiced even more about the success of 12 persons who gathered to study Dick

Westley's *Redemptive Intimacy*. Their thoughtful discussions involved everyone in the group and created new friendships among people who hungered for deeper links of relationship in the Church.

How involved were the adults themselves in shaping a program? Did a steering committee or the adult team decide on the topic and format and then work out the details of room arrangement, publicity and hospitality?

If so, consider the program successful in a different way. Bonding among the people who planned and shared responsibility for the program is a strong base for working relationships for future efforts.

Have you considered that some publicity may bring about a special success of its own—beyond drawing people to the program?

We invited an internationally known biblical scholar to our parish. Our team publicized the workshop well through newspaper ads, flyers, news articles and bulletin announcements. But we were disappointed and embarrassed over our crowd of only 100 people. Within six months, however, several churches of other denominations asked us to work with them on future co-sponsored events. They had recognized in our ads the high caliber of the speaker and the program we presented. The publicity led to interdenominational cooperation and an improved image of our church and Catholicism in general.

Did parishioners receive an image of a more hospitable Church through publicity about the programs?

One cannot underestimate the importance of sending a message to parish members about their value and about the care which the Church has for their ongoing faith development. We are aware that many feel alienated from the mainstream of parish life. We all have dark areas and painful wounds that need healing. Some may require time to trust the Church again—and may not come to any programs for a long time. Eventually, however, the invitations to "something more" may gradually wear down the barriers. In the meantime, these persons may continue to perceive in the programs offered a sense of welcome and care.

Did the team's hospitality and joy inspire a group of people to feel more alive and able to love?

Measuring this is difficult. We can only do it intuitively. Yet serving with love is itself a witness and a leaven within the community.

We must be careful of claiming too much responsibility for either the success or failure of programs. Above all, we must be wary of the temptation to blame people for not coming to certain events. Let's remember that we are working counter to centuries of Church history in which the laity took a more passive role. We are clearing new paths to an expanded concept of Church.

We will be most effective if we can focus on sowing abundantly, enjoying the act of planting without worrying about whether a shoot will spring up from each seed. We trust, instead, the Lord of the Harvest. As laborers we are called to pray through Jesus and work with him for that harvest.

We must challenge ourselves and each other to the work of re-visioning—seeing again what we have often looked at, clarifying what we are doing and hope to do. If we value only programs with standing-room-only crowds, we will be tempted often to discouragement. If, however, we value teamwork, collaboration between parishes, hospitality, personal interaction and ministry to the overlooked ones, we will hold within us a different vision of success—and gain a renewed respect and enthusiasm for our ministry.

Checklist

Do any of the programs reach a group of previously uninvolved people?

Do any programs build cooperation between parishes or between co-sponsoring groups within the parish?

Is the level of participation high in your programs? Are many questions asked? How much and what kind of interaction takes place?

68

Do you take responsibility for each program from its conception to evaluation? Do you learn something new from any "failure" that occurs?

Do you know any person who changed his or her mind or decided to live differently in some way because of any adult enrichment event?

Do you enjoy working with each other and creating a climate of friendliness and hospitality?

Author's Annotated Bibliography

DeBoy, James J. *Getting Started in Adult Religious Education.* New York: Paulist Press, 1979. A practical guide for beginners in adult religious education. Describes a system of evaluation on p. 98.

Powell, John and Loretta Brady. *The Fully Alive Experience.* Allen, Texas: Argus Press, 1980. A program of taped talks followed by group reflection. Designed to help people look at their attitudes as well as their need for change.

Westley, Dick. *Redemptive Intimacy.* Mystic, Conn.: Twenty-Third Publications, 1981. Challenges adults to look with new eyes at the implications of the Incarnation of Jesus. Excellent for group study. Discussion questions end each chapter.

CHAPTER NINE

Spirituality and the Adult Educator

PRAYER OF THE SELFISH CHILD

Now I lay me down to sleep,
I pray the Lord my soul to keep,
And if I die before I wake,
I pray the Lord my toys to break.
So none of the other kids can use 'em. . . .
Amen.

—Shel Silverstein, A Light in the Attic

If only I may grow: firmer, simpler—quieter, warmer.

—Dag Hammarskjold, Markings

No one wants to get stuck in prayer—or in life—at the stage of the selfish child in Silverstein's poem. As we grow, we learn to share. Much of our maturing process consists in learning to share more and more of our ideas, responsibilities, feelings, time, intimate thoughts, success and failure. We discover how to balance our needs with those of others, to reconcile our plans with the plans of others, to state our opinions and to let others challenge them. But then growth depends on how we respond to life's situations. How do we turn the successful and especially the potentially discouraging experiences into opportunities for ongoing spiritual and psychological growth? This chapter will discuss some of the ways.

Other adult education directors tell me that their most

frequent occasions of discouragement occur when facing breakdowns in communication, coping with power struggles, dealing with their own anger and resentment and handling time pressures. In a Hayes Associates workshop on conflict management for people in church settings, I learned that major problems facing many people in ministry are lack of honest communications, unwillingness to bargain or compromise, competitiveness for time, money and the use of church facilities and lack of self-esteem. These issues cross all denominational lines.

Conflicts resulting from faulty communications or interpersonal problems are part of any working environment. The adult team may experience blocks with members of the parish staff or with each other. Some people consistently squelch others' ideas and keep them from coming up for discussion. Some people may be able to offer creative suggestions for programs but not have the capacity to follow through with their share of the work needed to make them happen. Many well-meaning persons suffer from blind spots which prevent them from realizing the degree of frustration their behavior causes others.

Sponsoring a conflict management workshop or enlisting the help of a local counselor can facilitate open communication and better working relationships. Working together in harmony uses up far less energy and it increases enthusiasm and joy in the service of the community.

Between People by John Sanford is one of many excellent books which offer help in interpersonal skills. The author addresses root causes for communication failure and helps the reader move to a deeper understanding of how hidden agenda and emotions affect dialogue.

Owning Our Feelings

Leaders in adult education can be tempted to resent parishioners who do not take advantage of the special offerings the team has planned. One makes excuses for nonparticipation for just so long. "Why don't they see how good these programs are?" "Don't they care about their spiritual growth?" "Don't they realize that it is in being together that we are the people of God?" However these negative feelings surface, their theme is the same: Why don't they agree with us? Why don't they do what we think they should do?

If God calls us to support other persons in their faith journeys, we need to take our own seriously. That means dealing with the feelings inside of us—even those we don't want. At times we might be reluctant to confront the dark areas of ourselves that seem so unchristian. We shrink back when we find our true feelings so different from what we think a "real" follower of Christ would feel. In our inner struggle our thoughts may go something like this: "How can I help other people in their faith journeys when I am so far behind in mine? How can I help others if I'm feeling angry at them?"

We need to face openly our anger and resentment—and all of our feelings. Just admitting them helps to deflate some of their power to hurt us and the ministry.

Many of us have learned to deny our authentic responses in favor of what our culture and even some spiritual "experts" suggest we "should" feel. We can try to talk ourselves out of feeling angry or resentful by telling ourselves prematurely that the offending party did not intend any harm, but inwardly we continue to smoulder. Resentment, then, can be buried, but can surface in another way, such as non-cooperation, lack of warmth in personal dealings or resignation from the team due to "time pressures."

We need a way to process anger and resentments. Otherwise, they prevent our service to others from being life-giving encounters. Not only that, but unresolved anger can poison our spiritual and physical health. It can become a black hole, an energy drain pulling the flow of the Spirit's gifts down into it. Only in working through the feelings do we experience personal growth.

Many helpful books offer advice and ways to help process resentments. The late Anthony de Mello, S.J., recommends specific prayer exercises to enable people to move beyond anger and resentment to a deeper level of compassion and understanding. Prayer exercises 19 and 20 of *Sadhana, A Way to God* are especially useful. *Healing Life's Hurts* by Revs. Dennis and Matthew Linn takes the reader through a process of healing memories modeled on the work of Elizabeth Kubler-Ross's stages of death and dying. Among many audiocassettes the Revs. Linn have made on healing is *Prayer Course for Healing Life's Hurts*, published by Paulist Press.

Working Through Conflicts

While forgiving another, overlooking irritating behavior and working through anger to resolve it are often appropriate, at other times we need to deal with our anger by confronting the other person or group. When you have a sense that someone is being treated unjustly, then suffering in silence or turning the other cheek can be unchristian, an unloving thing to do.

In his book *Caring Enough Not to Forgive*, David Augsburger cautions against forgiving when one person has to do all the adjusting or absorb all the pain of a difficult situation. He advises Christians not to confuse a lack of assertiveness in themselves with true forgiveness. He writes: "When 'forgiveness' ends open relationships, leaves people cautious, twice shy, safely concealed, afraid to risk free open spontaneous living, don't forgive. It's not forgiveness. It's private alienation. It's individual estrangement."

Working through resentments one-sidedly gives the "forgiven" one permission to carry injustice even further. It widens the gap between mutuality. I found this happening in my parish when a group complained about some "liberal" books in the parish library. The controversy began with one book, *Christ Among Us*. Then the objectors, armed with materials from a right-wing Catholic organization, managed to find eight more books which they wanted to remove from our library shelves.

We published our library policy statement which declares that controversial books have a place in helping to clarify values. Including a book in the collection, it says, does not necessarily imply agreement with all of its contents. We also sought the help of our diocesan personnel, asking them to make a statement on the suitability of the books in question. The books remain on the shelves. If we had ignored the complaints, turned the other cheek and let the objecting group prevail, our entire library could have been jeopardized.

Managing Time

When programs multiply, so do responsibilities. Team members are frequently challenged to find time that doesn't seem to be available. Learning to manage time is essential to mental health, spiritual growth and quality of service.

A good handbook for time management is Jack Ferner's *Personal Guide to Time Management*. He suggests separating the week's time wheel into spaces for maintenance, personal growth, work, eating, sleeping and so on. This kind of book helps us face the fact that we cannot manufacture more than 24 hours a day, but we can *choose* how to spend the 24 hours we have. We can choose to take on tasks and we can choose to eliminate (many of) them. A generous person can spend a great deal of energy wondering why blowups are happening within the family, wondering why bursts of energy seem to be a thing of the past, or wondering why prayer seems flat and dull. The problem may be a mismanaged schedule, a time wheel badly in need of balancing. Loss of enthusiasm for ministry may also stem from lack of rest, physical exercise and general attention to our own physical health. A time chart can make us face the reality that we are not superhuman and that we need to set priorities and eliminate bottom items on the list.

Generous people who serve in ministry do so because they love the Church and want to give of themselves. This generosity can become an obstacle, however, when Church activities consume most of a person's leisure hours. Deciding where to draw the line is an individual matter. Families need to have time for each other, and team members need to cultivate interests beyond their ministry. Time wheels, reflection and prayer all help a person to decide how much time they can devote to ministry. Team members can help each other also by being sensitive to each other's needs for personal leisure. Don't hesitate to recommend that a team member take some time to be with family or friends. The team will be stronger for that kind of loving care.

Letting Go

Aesop's classic tale of the dog in the manger illustrates another pitfall common to Church ministry—possessive "love." In Aesop's tale, a dog jealously guards food from other animals without considering whether he can eat it all himself or whether the corn, oats and barley are even foods he can eat. His possessiveness takes over.

People usually rise to leadership because they exhibit valuable skills in organizing, speaking, teaching or working with groups. The danger for gifted people lies in thinking others cannot or will not do the job as well as they can. Or the leader trusts only her or his judgment and makes all the decisions alone. Leaders who become possessive of their ministries or their roles hoard all the "goodies" and others are not able to grow in developing their judgments and gifts.

The leader needs to model the kind of ministry he or she expects from others. The leader's love of people, which initiated the ministry in the first place, must be the generative love which parents experience when they wave good-bye to kids leaving home for college or their first jobs. As any parent who has ever shed a tear at having to make this break will tell you, nonpossessive love is not without its struggles. We always think we have something more to teach. Underneath lurks the feeling that the recipients of our loving care don't have the necessary skills to do it on their own. Or we are afraid they won't do it our way.

Jesus is our model for nonpossessive love. He does not guard all the roles, knowing he fills them better. He sends the disciples out as his spokespersons and eventually his replacements. He trusts that God will be with them, and he gracefully takes leave.

Learning to Listen

If we want to develop our relationships with family, friends or the people we serve, we need to develop our listening skills. Learning to hear people's feelings and their needs behind their words requires careful self-discipline and openness. Genuine listening allows other persons to experience their human depth in an atmosphere of Christlike love. It leads to self-acceptance and greater acceptance of others.

Spiritual masters like John of the Cross and Teresa of Avila have written eloquently of other spiritual disciplines such as frequent prayer, penance and participation in the sacraments. Listening as a spiritual discipline is just as demanding as any of these practices because it requires that we put aside any desire for power and influence and any thoughts of ourselves, our experience or our aspirations. We don't "solve" anything. We provide, instead, inner hospitality to whatever the other persons wish to reveal about themselves. We offer our readiness—even in helplessness—to be present to another.

A person who truly listens to another enters into a different sense of time. Less concerned with productivity and achieving goals, the listener "suspends" time and offers presence for the other. A good listener does not watch a clock but enters into the timeless world of the other's feelings and experiences. Listening is a rigorously demanding exercise, a gift of radical love. It can become balm for healing all kinds of problems, especially those of communication, anger, possessiveness and balance.

Our growth in the spiritual life has to do with more than praying, reading the Bible and helping the poor.

77

Growing as a person also happens through struggles—
struggles with communication, our own feelings, time and
ability to listen.

Trying to communicate more effectively and to handle
conflicts which arise can deepen our sense of community
and renew our time at Eucharist. In facing resentments, time
pressures and the need to control, we recognize our own
need for others to minister to us if we are to gain harmony in
our lives. These problems remind us how much we need the
kind of enrichment we are offering to others. Not a bad
insight for an adult educator.

Checklist

Do you monitor your attitude toward those who rarely
or never attend any of the events you planned?

Do you have a way to deal with feelings of anger or
resentments that surface within this work?

Can you communicate the conflict, hurt feelings and
resentments to the person who is the source of the
frustration?

Do you come to terms with your limits by setting a
realistic timelog?

Are you paying attention to your health—the need for
adequate sleep, nutrition and balance in your daily
routine?

Have you made some effort to recognize when you are
loving your ministry possessively?

Can you see the value of working through the struggles
of this ministry as a discipline on the way to personal
growth?

Did anyone on the team attend a workshop or read a book on:

1) conflict management?

2) handling time pressures?

3) healing old hurts?

4) dealing with present anger?

5) interpersonal skills?

6) listening skills?

7) prayer?

Author's Annotated Bibliography

Augsburger, David. *Caring Enough to Forgive: Caring Enough to Not Forgive.* Ventura, Calif.: Regal Books, 1981. Short, thoughtful book on when forgiveness is appropriate and when it is not.

DeMello, Anthony, S.J. *Sadhana: A Way to God.* St. Louis: The Institute of Jesuit Sources, 1979. A wide choice of prayer forms adapted from both Eastern sources and Christian tradition. The book is designed to be prayed through rather than read.

Ferner, Jack. *Successful Time Management.* New York: John Wiley and Sons, 1980. A complete, self-teaching guide to gaining control of time. It comes complete with sample worksheets, forms and planning guides.

Groeschel, Benedict J. *Spiritual Passages.* New York: Crossroad Publishing Company, 1984. Weds contemporary psychology with theories of traditional spiritual development for a balanced view of growth issues that affect modern Christians.

Lee, James Michael. *The Spirituality of the Religious Educator.* Birmingham, Ala.: Religious Education Press, 1985. A collection of essays. Some interesting thoughts on the nature of spirituality by Randolph Crump Miller.

Linn, Dennis and Linn, Matthew. *Healing Life's Hurts: Healing Memories Through Five Stages of Forgiveness.* New York: Paulist Press, 1978. Method of dealing with hurt and resentment based on the work of Elizabeth Kubler-Ross.

Sanford, John. *Between People.* New York: Paulist Press, 1982. Examines communication and relationship and the power of creative listening, among other topics.

Schmidt, Joseph F. *Praying Our Experiences.* Winona, Minn.: Christian Brothers Publications, 1981. A tiny gem of a book on the challenge of identifying prayer in the lives of busy people.

Vanderwall, Francis W. *Water in the Wilderness.* Mahwah, N.J.: Paulist Press, 1985. Helpful and practical guide for those wishing to deepen their prayer lives. Includes specific forms of prayer and offers the busy person many options in prayer methods. Tone is reassuring and sensitive to the hectic pace of modern life.

Afterword

While the image of the "simple faithful" might have nostalgic charm for some people, we cannot afford to postpone the adult education movement in the Church any longer. Today's Catholics increasingly will need to bring their own Church experience in line with the intelligent and competent roles they fill in secular society.

Demographics tell us that tomorrow's Church will have significantly fewer clergy. We will not have the luxury of allowing "Father" to do most of the ministry in the Church. If people in parishes are to prepare for real leadership, they must have opportunities right in their own parishes for real learning, for nurturing their spirits and for reflection on what a faith commitment means. Church documents call laity to become partners in sharing the ministry of the Church.

The diminishing numbers of clergy present an exciting challenge to both priests and laypeople today. Priests will need to overcome any fear of welcoming lay women and men as decision-makers in the Church. Pastors will need to know their people well in order to invite them to become partners in ministry, responsible for helping shape their own continuing education in the faith. Laypeople will need for priests to say, "You have important skills that our Church needs. Will you help?"

People in the Church of the future will need to be generous with their time, not at the expense of their families, but to extend that care beyond significant others to a wider family of humankind. They also will need to take time to nourish their spirits with information and inspiration. The role of adult educator is a prophetic one which invites adults away from the privacy of isolated lives and into participation with a community of pilgrims from deep places within our spirits.

I believe that some of the program ideas, resources and suggestions in these pages will help parish groups in adult education work. Through your letters, I hope that many of you will share with me the good news of your ministry.

But we are sure in your regard, beloved, of better things related to salvation, even though we speak in this way. For God is not unjust so as to overlook your work and the love you have demonstrated for his name by having served and continuing to serve the holy ones. We earnestly desire each of you to demonstrate the same eagerness for the fulfillment of hope until the end, so that you may not become sluggish, but imitators of those who, through faith and patience, are inheriting the promises (Hebrews 6:9-12).

Sample Evaluation Form

Program Title

How did you find out about this program?

- ☐ brochure/flyer
- ☐ newspaper advertisement
- ☐ bulletin announcement
- ☐ Sunday Mass announcement
- ☐ friend/parishioner
- ☐ other _____

Did you feel welcome at this program? If not, why?

Was the program time convenient for you? If not, what time is convenient for you?

Did the program meet the following goals? Circle your response for each goal listed.

goal 1 _____ Yes No

goal 2 _____ Yes No

goal 3 _____ Yes No

What did you like most about this program?

What did you like least about this program?

Is there anything this program should have included?

Did you learn anything new from this program?

Did the program inspire you to a new course of action in your life or to modify your opinion in any way? If so, how?

Was there ample opportunity for you to ask questions and share your views and experience?

What suggestions would you have for future programs?

Would you like to be on our mailing list for future adult faith development programs?

Do you know anyone else who would like to be on our mailing list? Please give us their names, addresses and phone numbers.

Do you have any additional comments?

Optional

Name _____

Address _____

City _____

State _____ Zip _____

Telephone _____(day) _____ (evening)

Resource Guide

Author's Annotated Bibliography

Bossart, Donald E. *Creative Conflict in Religious Education and Church Administration*. Birmingham, Ala.: Religious Education Press, 1980. An unusual approach to the positive value of conflict in the Church. Includes specific plans for structuring conflict as a learning tool in religious education classes.

Boys, Mary C., ed. *Ministry and Education in Conversation*. Winona, Minn.: St. Mary's Press, 1981. A challenging series of articles sketching a vision for the adult educator as minister and educator. Includes essays by Sandra Schneiders, Sara Butler and others.

Parent, Neil A., ed. *Christian Adulthood: A Catechetical Resource, 1983*. Washington, D.C.: United States Catholic Conference, 1982 (and subsequent years). A helpful collection of articles, from theoretical foundations, program development, leadership and professional development and resources. Articles tend to be well written and practical, with a number of specific "how-to" questions addressed. Published annually.

Schaefer, James R. *The Parish Adult Education Team*. Baltimore, Md.: Divisions of Adult Religious Education, 1975. A 15-page pamphlet to orient the adult education team to their mission in the parish. Includes information on how the team relates to other parish groups.

Simon, Sidney. *Getting Unstuck*. New York: Warner Books, 1988. Focuses on breaking down our innate resistance to change. Author offers methods for maintaining flexibility in our relationships and life-styles.

Stokes, Kenneth. *Faith Is a Verb*. Mystic, Conn.: Twenty-Third Publications, 1989. Among the issues discussed: whether or not there are "stages" of faith development, the role of doubt as a positive element in adult growth and the distinction between "religious" and "spiritual."

Walsh, Eugene A. *Talking with Adults: Practical Suggestions for Preaching, Teaching, Evangelizing*. Glendale, Ariz.: Pastoral Arts Associates of North America, 1980. A wonderful burst of theology geared to the language and life-experience of contemporary adults. Includes such topics as talking with adults about God, Jesus, spirit, faith, prayer, sin and reconciliation in words people understand.

Other General Resources

Chilson, Richard. *Prayermaking*. Minneapolis, Minn.: Winston Press, 1977. Offers advice about avenues of spiritual growth not always found in conventional books on spirituality. Author's humor and expertise in Eastern spirituality offer the reader more choices for deepening self-understanding and awareness.

From Ashes to Easter. Washington, D.C.: The Liturgical Conference, 1979. This was our primary resource for "the breaking of the word" during Lent. It is designed as a study guide based on the Sunday liturgical readings. Includes all three cycles of readings.

Genesis II, the original program in 18 sessions. The original printed materials are available from The Center for Human Development, P.O. Box 4557, Washington, D.C. 20017, (202)529-7724. The original films are available on one videocassette from Tabor Publishing, P.O. Box 7000, Allen, TX 75002. Tabor Publishing also offers an abbreviated form of the Genesis II program.

Jay, Antony. "How to Run a Meeting," *Harvard Business Review*, March-April 1976. A humorous article on how to make meetings efficient and effective.

Organizations

Evangelization

The Paulist National Catholic Evangelization Association, 3031 Fourth St., N.E., Washington, DC 20017, (202)832-5022. Publishes a newsletter, *Conversion,* six times each year. It describes ways of reaching out to alienated Catholics and the unchurched and of bringing interested persons into the Catholic Church. Also sponsors RCIA workshops and evangelization conferences and publishes *Share the Word,* a low-cost, flexible Bible study program based on the Sunday Scripture readings.

National Office of RENEW, 1232 George St., Plainfield, NJ 07062, (201)769-5400. RENEW is a program (usually diocesan-wide) for personal and parish renewal based on praying and studying the Scriptures. A three-year process with two six-week segments each year. Carefully thought out and well planned.

U.S. Catholic Conference, 3211 Fourth St., N.E., Washington, DC 20017-1194, (800)235-8722. The USCC publishes both official Vatican documents and bishops' statements on a wide range of topics. They also commission special studies in adult education work and parish life. Their Standing Order Service is a quarterly mailing of the most current documents. They have a subscription service which offers a 40-percent discount on all USCC publications to subscribers. For an adult library, the Standing Order Service can be a good investment.

Lay Ministry

National Association for Lay Ministry, 1125 West Baseline Rd., Suite 2-67, Mesa, AZ 85210, (602)839-9785. An organization designed to promote the universal call to ministry, to support those involved in the work of lay ministry, to foster research and development within the field. Sponsors an annual national conference and network with other groups to support the lay vocation.

Spirituality

National Pastoral Life Center, 299 Elizabeth St., New York, NY 10012, (212)431-7825. The Center is affiliated with the USCC and is devoted to the development of parish life. Provides information, training, consultation.

Retreats International, P.O. Box 1067, Notre Dame, IN 46556, (219)239-5320. Sponsors one of the most varied summer programs for those who wish to deepen their spiritual life and learn at the same time. Top names in the field of spirituality and social justice.

Spiritual Book Associates, Notre Dame, IN 46556, (219)287-2838. Publishes a bimonthly newsletter with book reviews and information on what is current in the field of spiritual writing.

Catalogs

The following publishers specialize in religious education materials. Their catalogs, which are free, offer brief descriptions of the materials. They are useful in building a library and media center and in planning programs using films or videotape.

Abbey Press, 161 Hill Dr., St. Meinrad, IN 47577, (812)357-8220. Primarily a gift catalog, Abbey also includes some family life resources, posters, cards and bookmarks.

ACTA Foundation, 4848 North Clark St., Chicago, IL 60640, (312)271-1030. Excellent filmstrips on the Bible.

Affirmation Books, 9 Spring St., Whitingsville, MA 01588, (617)234-6266. Catalog carries a wide variety of books and tapes on psychologically oriented material for people in pastoral or parish ministry.

Alba House Communications, 9531 Akron-Canfield Road, P.O. Box 595, Canfield, OH 44406-0595, (800)533-2522. Offers variety of books and tapes, including the tape series "Issues in Bio-medical Ethics" and "Paul's Community, and Christians and Jews."

Alternatives Bookstore, P.O. Box 429, Ellenwood, GA 30049, (404)961-0102. Peace and justice materials. Many effective discussion tools for adult groups.

Argus Communications, One DLM Park, P.O. Box 5000, Allen, TX 75002, (800)527-4748. Resources aimed at confirmation-age youth. Also materials developed by psychologist Rev. John Powell.

Autom, 2226 North Seventh St., Phoenix, AZ 85006, (602)258-8481. A wide range of religious books. Sales periodically offer savings of 50 percent off regular price.

Ave Maria Press, Notre Dame, IN 46556, (219)287-2831. Offers prayer books, books on spirituality, pastoral problems. Discounts of 20 percent for orders over $100.00.

Baker Book House, P.O. Box 6287, Grand Rapids, MI 49506, (616)676-9185. Catalog includes bargain items in most religious areas.

William C. Brown Group, 2460 Kerper Blvd., Dubuque, IA 52001, (319)588-1451, (Northwest Office). A catalog with some textbooks and materials for adult learners.

Channing L. Bete Company, Inc., 200 State Rd., South Deerfield, MA 01373, (800)628-7733. A series of "scriptographic booklets" are offered which treat subjects like, "How the Bible Came to Be," "What Makes a Catholic?"

"What Is the RCIA?" in a light, brief manner. Booklets average 20 pages.

Charismatic Renewal Services, 237 North Michigan St., South Bend, IN 46601, (219)234-6021. Books on Scripture, family life, spirituality. Also some records, plaques and medals.

Clergy Book Service, 12855 West Silver Spring Dr., Butler, WI 53007, (800)558-0580. Offers a discount service on religious titles and publishes a monthly newsletter *Bookviews* which reviews current titles.

The Communication Center, P.O. Box 4458, South Bend, IN 46634, (800)348-2227. Discount Catholic book distributor. Ships within 24 to 36 hours. Normally a 20 percent discount. Can procure any book or tape in print.

Demco Bound Books, P.O. Box 7488, Madison, WI 53707, (800)356-8394. Offers a wide selection of religious and nonreligious books in special bindings for libraries.

Franciscan Communications, 1229 South Santee St., Los Angeles, CA 90015, (213)746-2916. Wide variety of audiovisual materials, including videotape series, posters, banners, certificates and booklets for pastoral visiting.

Graymoor Ecumenical Institute, 475 Riverside Dr., New York, NY 10115, (914)424-3183. Publishes sample prayer services for the interfaith celebration of the Week of Prayer for Christian Unity during the third week in January.

Ignatius Press, 2515 McAllister St., San Francisco, CA 94118, (800)322-1531. Publishes some helpful Church documents.

Institute of Jesuit Sources, 3700 West Pine Blvd., St. Louis, MO 63108, (314)652-5737. Catalog of books related to Ignatian spirituality.

The Jesuit Educational Center for Human Development, 42 Kirkland St., Cambridge, MA 02138, (617)547-1250. Publishes *Human Development* with excellent articles for the pastoral counselor. Also offers a variety of referral services for mental health cases. They also offer a small catalog of other publications in pastoral counseling.

Ligouri Publications, One Ligouri Dr., Ligouri, MO 63057, (800)325-9521. Some catechetical aids and a few religious titles for general reading.

Liturgy Training Publications, Archdiocese of Chicago, 1800 North Hermitage Ave., Chicago, IL 60622-1101, (312)486-8970. Well-written and affordable, this collection of booklets covers areas from RCIA sponsor training to planning for weddings and funerals. A useful catalog.

Loyola University Press, 3441 North Ashland Ave., Chicago, IL 60657, (800)621-1008. Small selection of books which usually have some connection to Jesuit history or spirituality.

LuraMedia Gift Catalog, P.O. Box 261668, San Diego, CA 92126-0998, (800)367-5872. Out-of-the-ordinary books and posters.

Mass Media Ministries, 2116 North Charles St., Baltimore, MD 21218, (301)727-3270. Excellent film catalog with special seasonal films for Advent, Lent and Christmas.

NCR Credence Cassettes, 115 East Armour Blvd., Kansas City, MO 64111, (800)444-8910. Large selection of audiocassette programs. Discounts offered.

Orbis Books, Walsh Bldg., Maryknoll, NY 10545, (800)258-5838. On request Orbis will photocopy and bind specialized studies from either author-prepared typescripts or books not available in the United States. Offers many books on social justice themes.

Paulist Press, 997 Macarthur Blvd., Mahwah, NJ 07430, (201)825-7300. A wide selection of topics ranging from spirituality to doctrine. Some video cassettes. Publishes *Service*, quarterly resources for parish liturgy and pastoral ministry. Catalog published every two months. Occasional special catalog for religious education sales and scholarly books.

Paulist Productions INSIGHT Films, P.O. Box 1057, Pacific Palisades, CA 90272, (800)624-8613. Excellent collection of films on growth issues—parenting, alcoholism, divorce, feminine spirituality, sexuality.

The Printery House, Conception Abbey, Conception, MO 64433, (816) 944-2331. Catalog includes some books, cards, plaques, medals and posters.

Religious Education Press, 5316 Meadow Brook Rd., Birmingham, AL 35243, (205)991-1000. Publishes a handful of very fine books on religious education topics.

ROA Media, 2460 Kerper Blvd., Dubuque, IA 52001, (319)588-1451. A wide selection of films on parenting, values clarification, comedy, human rights, Scripture.

St. Anthony Messenger Press, 1615 Republic St., Cincinnati, OH 45210, (800)336-1770. Publishes *Catholic Update*, books and audiocassettes. *Updates* give brief, to-the-point information in an affordable and visually appealing format.

Twenty-Third Publications, P.O. Box 180, Mystic, CT 06355, (800)321-0411. Publishes *Today's Parish*, a monthly periodical with helpful ideas for parish ministry. Also offers a catalog of books on practical aspects of Christian living.

Winston Press, P.O. Box 1630, Hagerstown, MD 21741, (800)328-5125. Offers some video programs as well as challenging books for adult discussion groups on biblical subjects, spirituality and parish ministry.